I0146578

Co-Edited and Compiled by: Linda J Speck Schwientek

Co-Edited by: Sarah Finch

Thumbs Up Publications

Printed in Canada

ISBN: 978-0-9936318-3-2

Published 2016

2014-15 Snapshot

Our Family

Our Friends

Our Home

Our Neighbours

2014-15 Snapshot

Events to Remember

What happens today...

Will be history tomorrow.

2014 Headlines

Olympics

The 2014 Winter Olympics, officially called the XXII Olympic Winter Games were held in February in Sochi, Krasnodar Krai, Russia.
A total of 98 events in 15 winter sport disciplines were held during the Games.

Frozen Falls

The frigid temperatures brought on by the polar vortex, in the winter of 2014 saw parts of Niagara Falls came to a standstill as the waters literally froze in place as they fell.
Many beautiful photos were captured and posted online. Photos of the falls were reported on around the world.

Hockey

Both the Canadian men's and women's hocket teams won gold medals at the Olympics. The women beat the USA 3-2 winning the Olympic gold medal. The men's team won their gold, beating Sweden 3-0.

Apple

Apple unveils larger smartphones the iPhone 6 models, a smartwatch and mobile payments. It was amid questions over whether the company still has a knack for innovation following the 2011 death of co-founder Steve Jobs.

Crops

Because of a wet, cold spring and a so-so summer, the soybean harvest is late, a good chunk of the winter wheat may never get planted, and some farmers may gamble on not harvesting their late-planted corn until spring.

2015 Headlines

Syria

January, 7, 2015 it was announced that Canada will resettle 10,000 more Syrian refugees over the next three years in direct response to the United Nations Refugee Agency's global appeal to resettle 100,000 refugees worldwide.

Cuba & US

On July 20, 2015, Cuba and the United States reestablish full diplomatic relations, ending a 54-year stretch of hostility between the nations.

Climate

A global climate change pact is agreed at the COP 21 summit, held in December 2015, committing all countries to reduce carbon emissions for the first time.

NASA

NASA announces that liquid water has been found on Mars on September 28, 2015.

Trudeau

After leading the Liberal Party to a resounding majority win in Canada's 42nd general election, held October 19, 2015, prime minister-designate Justin Trudeau was featured in headlines around the world. Trudeau, the second-youngest Canadian prime minister in history is also the the eldest son of former Prime Minister Pierre Trudeau, the first child of a previous prime minister to hold the post.

Late Night

After 33 years in late-night television and more than 4,600 "Top Ten Lists," David Letterman retired from CBS's Late Show with David Letterman on May 20, 2015. And with that (and Jay Leno's second departure from The Tonight Show in 2014), it truly was the end of an era for television.

ZORRA TOWNSHIP

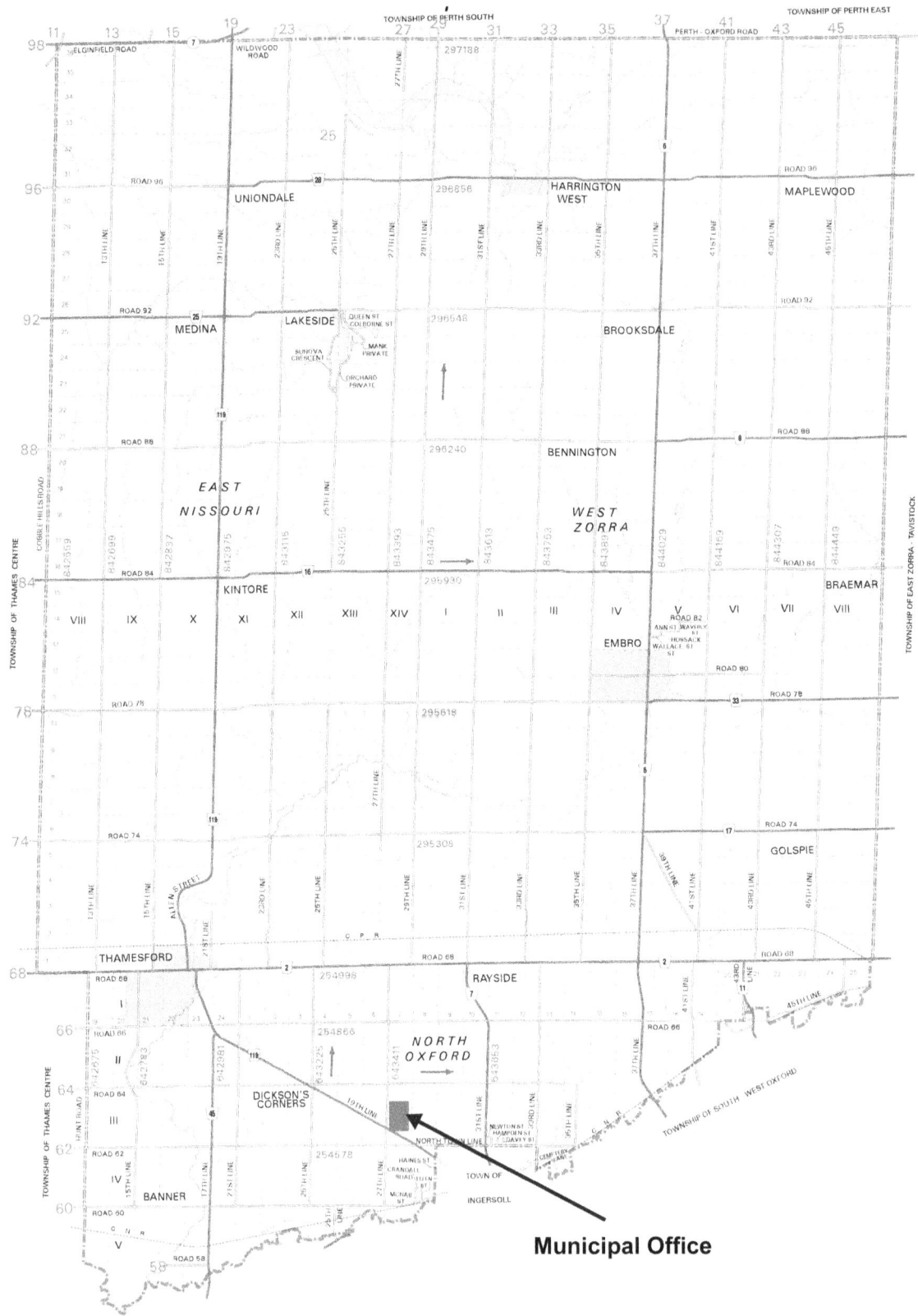

Municipal Office

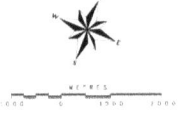

Table of Contents

Family Stories

West 1

Van Egdom 2

Hodgins 3

Oliver 4

Clark 8

Innes 10

Adams 12

Sports 14

Zorra Township 16

Embro 35

Thamesford 51

Kintore 74

Lakeside 80

Harrington 88

Uniondale 89

Military 90

Schools 98

Agriculture 116

Zorra Township
A rural municipality located at the north-west corner of Oxford County.
The Township is comprised of several rural clusters and two serviced villages.
The population of Zorra Township is 8,125,
with a total land area of 529 square kilometers.

Family Stories

WEST FAMILY
Melvin (b. 1922) and Lila (Kittmer) West

Lila and Melvin West

*Lila with her granddaughter Emily
during the summer of 1989*

Melvin and Lila West moved to 7 Commissioner St., Pt. Lot 11, Con. 4, Embro from Lot 10, Con. 1 on July 1, 1979.

Mel had retired from farming in 1981, and enjoyed moving to their house in a maple wooded lot in Embro.

Mel had lived in Chesley and always cut wood and made maple syrup in his spare time, so this spot in Embro was perfect.

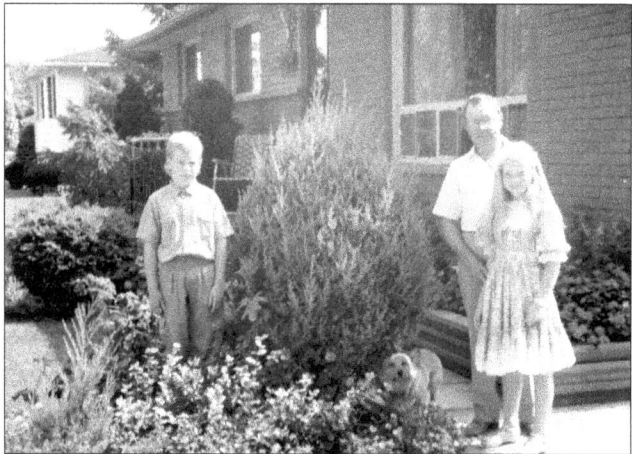

*Mel poses with his grandson, Adam and
granddaughter, Emily in 1989*

In 1983 Lila retired from teaching at Zorra Highland Park School outside of Embro.

In that same year she and Mel severed a building lot on the west side of their property for their daughter Mary and her husband Harry Van Egdom.

The Wests enjoyed flowers and gardening. Mel was known to pick raspberries for hours in his large berry patch. If you saw the Wests you could be sure there was a corgie, their dog of choice, nearby!

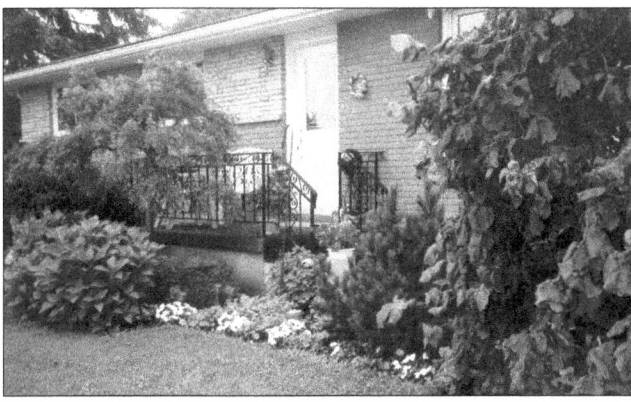

*Lila and Melvin West's home located at
7 Commissioner St., Pt. Lot 11, Con. 4, Embro*

VAN EGDOM FAMILY
Harry and Mary (West)

Harry and Mary (West) Van Egdom moved to 3 Commissioner St., Part Lot 11, Con 4, Embro from Lot 10, Con. 3 Commissioner St., Part Lot 11, Con 4, Embro in October 1988.

Harry was a dairy farmer and Mary had her own hairdressing shop on the farm. They have two children Adam (b. 1980) and Emily (b. 1983).

Due to a farm accident, Harry lost his right leg and was forced to sell the farm. They purchased the wooded property from Mary's parents, Melvin and Lila West.

In the spring of 1988, trees were removed and major excavating and building started. M&R Construction of Embro built their lovely red brick home.

Harry, Mary, Adam and Emily Van Egdom, 1993

Van Egdom Family, 2008

Harry and Mary Van Egdom's home located at 3 Commissioner St., Pt. Lot 11, Con. 4, Embro

Harry is working in farm related sales and Mary changed from hair to feet. She is a pedicurist. Both of their children were married in 2010.

Adam and Mandy live in Beachville. They have a son, Spencer born March 29, 2015. Emily and Phil have a son, Logan born June 20, 2012 and a daughter Lila, born March 18, 2015. They bought Emily's grandparents, Mel and Lila West's home in Embro.

Harry and Mary Van Egdom, Phil, Emily, Logan and Lila Hodgins, Adam, Mandy and Spencer Van Egdom

HODGINS FAMILY
Phillip and Emily (Van Egdom)

Philip and Emily Hodgins bought the property of 7 Commissioner St., Part Lot 11, Con. 4, Embro in November 2009 from Melvin and Lila West, Emily's grandparents.

Phil and Emily were married on August 14, 2010 at Knox United Church in Embro.

Phil works as a mechanical engineering technologist at Pow Engineering in Ingersoll. Emily is a teacher at Innerkip Public School.

On June 20, 2012, Phil and Emily had a baby boy, Logan. Logan loves running around outside with his Scotty dog, Izzy. On March 18, 2015, Phil and Emily welcomed a baby girl, Lila. Lila loves trying to keep up with her brother.

Many renovations have been done to the interior and exterior of this home. The Hodgins family loves living in Embro and making memories in their home.

The Hodgins' family home

Phil, Logan, Emily and Lila Hodgins

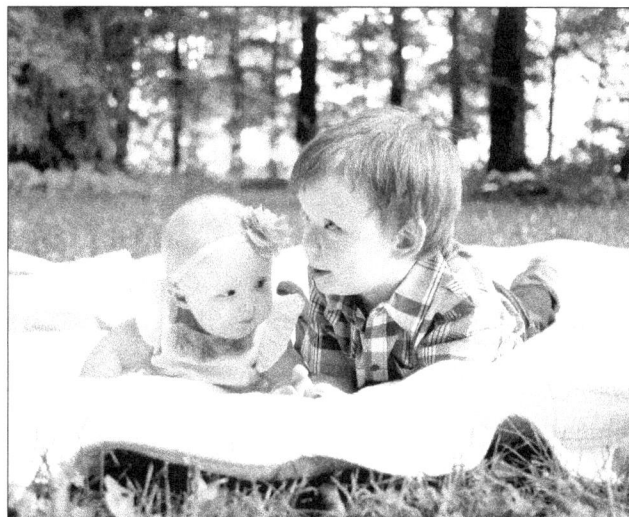

Logan and Lila Hodgins

OLIVER FAMILY
My Brother Tommy
By Anne Matheson

I call him Tommy because of all our childhood memories. I remember the day that Mom and Dad brought Tommy home from the hospital. The rest of us kids were only allowed a short glimpse of this little guy all bundled up with a full head of bright red hair.

Tommy is the seventh child and the fifth son of my parents Francis and Jean Oliver. He was born in March 1955. Back in those days, mothers stayed in hospital for 12 days after having a baby. Yes, things were different sixty years ago.

We lived on the 6th Concession, Lot 20 of what was then known as West Zorra. My Mother and Dad farmed with my Grandfather and Grandmother Oliver. We had cows, horses and chickens but our main stay was growing and selling vegetables. It was a family affair. We all helped plant, harvest and sell the vegetables at three markets every Saturday morning. Guess that's where we learned that a little hard work never hurt us and when you work hard, it is very rewarding.

As well as working, we all played together, whether it was skating, sports, music, board games or swimming at the local Symons Creek, we were never apart for long. My sister and youngest brother Tommy took piano lessons together and I'll never forget playing a trio with them. The song was Johnny's So Long at the Fair. The three of us also sang in the Hickson United Church Choir. This is where we discovered that Tommy could sing, and sing very well. Mom took him to voice lessons in Stratford from a Mr. Scott. He began singing for weddings and shows at school.

His first public school performance was at Zorra Highland Park School when they performed the Sound of Music. Tommy played the part of Captain Von Trapp. The show was a hit and they filled the school gym over and over again and had to put on extra shows to accommodate everyone. We were so proud of him.

At Woodstock Collegiate Institute high school he met Fran Potter who also could sing very well. They sang together at many functions throughout Oxford County. They produced a benefit show to raise money for

Francis and Jean Oliver and family

Muscular Dystrophy which afflicted our brother Eddie. Many other local people performed at this concert which was a sell out at the W.C.I. Auditorium. I still remember one of the acts, our piano teacher and organist Norma Rowe from Hickson playing the theme song from "The Sting". Everyone raved about the show and the wonderful local talent in Oxford County. Tom and Fran were invited to perform at the Royal Winter Fair, which I was lucky enough to go see.

My brother Tom studied hard at music schools across the country and sang with the Canadian Opera Company for a while but it was tough going. Tom has a baritone voice, actually a lyrical baritone and the big parts in the operas always went to a higher tenor men's voice. He then decided to get his Bachelor of Music to teach voice. He now lives in Hamilton and runs his own voice studio called Voice Concepts, which has become very successful throughout the Toronto area by coaching up and coming opera stars. If you google Voice Concepts you can see more about my little brother Tommy.

"In Touch With Tom"

featuring

TOM OLIVER

along with PHYLLIS BARTLEY

TOM CLARK   WCI CHOIR
& BRUCE JAKEMAN   & MANY OTHERS

Saturday May 15, 1976 8:00 pm

Proceeds to Muscular Dystrophy Assoc. of Canada

ADULTS $2.00   STUDENTS $1.00

Tom Oliver at mike with Phyllis Bartley at the piano (Staff photo)

Variety night a success

Mayor Les Cook signs a proclamation making
Muscular Dystrophy Week May 8-15 official in Woodstock.
Tom Oliver, the producer of an upcoming variety show
in aid of MD looks on.

TOM & FRAN

Present . . .

"Believe In Music '74"

TOM OLIVER AND FRAN POTTER

Couple will sing at pageant for Miss Dominion of Canada

By MILLY TAYLOR
Sentinel-Review
Family Editor

From their first appearance singing together two years ago at WCI Fran Potter and Tom Oliver have come a long way. The couple were asked by John Bruno at Happy Tap to sing at the July 1 Miss Dominion of Canada Pageant at the Sheridan Brock.

It is in the form of a cabaaret style with tables situated around the auditorium that will seat approximately 1000 people.

FRAN AND TOM

Unfortunately it will not be televised buy anyone may attend by purchasing tickets for a minimum fee at the door.

There will be 18 to 24 girls participating from across Canada ranging in ages of 18-26 to compete in beauty, poise and personality.

Miss Dominion of Canada sends one representative to Miss Universe contest which will be held in July in South America this year.

Fran and Tom will be singing songs that range from "Side by Side" to modern day music like, "We've Only Just Begun."

They will travel to Toronto for rehearsal on June 30. A professional organist will accompany them during the pageant.

"This is a real challenge for us. It will be the first time there won't be a lot of our friends in the audience," said Tom.

For Fran her musical career began at age three when she sang at church. She was in the music festval from Grade one on. She took piano from Marie Thomson and vocal from Ruth Hodgins and has Grade nine in vocal.

Presently she and Tom take vocal lessons from Gordon Scott of Stratford. Fran is a graduate of Grade 13, WCI and has spent the past year studying music.

Tom has his Grade 10 in vocal and a basic background in piano from Norma Rowe. Tom will be returning to WCI next year to complete Grade 13.

They are usually attending different functions to sing three times a week and enjoy meeting people. They have appeared at anniversary services at churches, garden parties, annual dinners, weddings and for the past 2 years have put on a show for Muscular Dystrophy at WCI raising $1162. in 1973 and over $1100. this year. They added how greatly they appreciated John Bowman of London who was MC for the show for both years and who helped with stage directions.

They both enjoy music and going to variety shows and dances.

Fran is registrar for Camp Bimini this year and Tom is involved with the camp's work. Both are members of Junior Farmers. Two years ago Tom won the Male Vocol solo for Oxford County through the Junior Farmers competition.

Fran teaches CGIT at Dundas Street United Church.

They travelled with the WCI school choir all over Oxford County singing, accompanied by Clarence Orton.

Both Fran and Tom praised their school teachers for entering them in school festivals when they were younger. It helped them get accustomed to getting in front of an audience.

In closing they said, "We owe so much to our parents for their unselfish donation of time and money, their helpful suggestions and their tremendous support."

Two published articles about Tom and his career.

Tom Oliver was born in Embro, ON south of Stratford. After his education at the Royal Conservatory of Music, he continued his music education at the Banff School of Fine Arts & The San Francisco Conservatory of Music where he completed his Honours B.A. in Voice Performance in 1982. Tom's professional education includes The Mastery Leadership and Neuro-Linguistic training from the Actors Institute in Los Angeles. In 1985, Tom developed two ten-week voice training programs for the Actors Studio 58 at Langara College in Vancouver. Along with his work in film and television, Tom has appeared as solo artist with the Sacremento Opera, Vancouver Opera and Symphony, Edmonton Opera Touring Co., Winnipeg Rainbow Stage, Opera Piccola and the Canadian Opera Company.

Tom left performing in 1993 to continue his research in voice. Currently living and teaching in Toronto, he provides the community with a unique and rewarding approach to vocal training and expression. Finding and developing the dominant sense of one's expression is a key part in Tom's research and studio work.

TOM OLIVER Early in life Tom figured out that it was easier to compete in vocal competitions than to assist his six siblings weed parsnips on the homestead, Olivers' Gardens in Embro Ontario. This avoidance led to music scholarship and more education. On completion of his education at the **Royal Conservatory of Music in Toronto,** he continued on to the **Banff School of Fine Arts** and the **San Francisco Conservatory of Music** where he completed his **Honours in Voice Performance** in 1982.

Principal soloist contracts include: **The Sacramento Opera, The Vancouver Opera and Symphony, The Edmonton Opera Touring Company, The Winnipeg Rainbow Stage, Canada Opera Picola and The Canadian Opera Company.**
He produced and performed two concerts for **Mrs. Mila Mulroney:** Post dinner concert at the **World Summit** in Vancouver and again in Toronto the **First Lady's** post dinner concert for **U.S. First Lady Nancy Reagan.**

In **1993,** he left performing professionally to continue his research in voice. Currently living and teaching from his private studio, **Voice Concepts,** in Toronto, he provides the community with a unique and rewarding approach to vocal training and expression. This led to **Voices In The Night....**which serves not only as a performing opportunity for students but also as an opportunity to contribute. Over 50 concerts and 80,000 charity dollars later, Tom is simply amazed what **avoiding a few parsnips** can do!

CLARK FAMILY

The Clark family homestead located on the corner of Dundas and Middleton Streets in Thamesford dates back to 1894.

John Andrew 'Jack' Clark, a son of James Clark and Sarah Dundas Clark of North Oxford, purchased 1, 2, 3, 4 of L-22, C 1 fronting the south side of Dundas St. and the north side of Brock St., plus parcels 1, 2, 3, 4 of L-21 C1 on the south side of Brock St. in North Oxford from the estate of Alexander Draffin for $625 on May 6, 1893.

Jack was a carpenter, building houses and barns. He built his own house on corner of Dundas and Middleton St. in 1894. He was married in May 1895 to Letitia Jane Day, daughter of a former warden of Oxford County, Matthew Joseph Day.

Upon Jack's death in 1929, Letitia opened up her house as a tourist home. One time she played hostess to The Dumbells, an entertainment group started up in WWI to entertain the troops. *See more about the Dumbells at the end of the military section*.

Jack and Letitia Clark had three sons, Robert Sterling, Mervyn Franklin and John Howard.

Robert owned and operated R.S. Clark & Son Sand & Gravel in Ingersoll, Ontario.

Letitia and Jack Clark

Mervyn was general manager of White Trucks out of Buffalo, NY.

John was a bank clerk for the Royal Bank, Parts Manager for G.G. Hogg Ford dealership in Thamesford and clerk for the Police Village of Thamesford plus treasurer for the local branch of the Ontario Hydro Electric System.

Clark house located on the corner of Dundas and Middleton Streets in Thamesford

Coza and Howard Clark

Clark house barn

Howard married Coza Truefitt in 1935 and they had three daughters, Gail, Sandra and Alana.

Howard obtained the family property on the corner of Dundas and Middleton Street in 1941, preceding Letitia's death. He sold parcels 1, 2, 3, 4 on the North and South of Brock Street in 1951 to Matheson's Farm Equipment dealership.

Howard died in 1960 and Coza lived on the property until her death in 2009.

The property was sold to Tom Willis in 2010.

Gail Vyse, Howard and Coza's oldest daughter, continues to live in Thamesford.

Clark house restored by Tom and Diane Willis

INNES FAMILY

Con 5 Lot 28

Information from the 1871 census lists:

Alexander Innes, age 37,
Barbara (McLean), age 35,
Margaret, age 12 (married Fedwich Duncan),
Mary, age 10,
Isobella, age 7 (married James Green),
Barbara, age 4,
James, age 2.

Church records lists James Green and Isobella's marriage as occurring on December 1884. The witnesses were William Innes and Mary Green. Possibly these two were first cousins of Isobella's. The son and daughter of William Innes, Alexander's brother who farmed 1/2 a mile north of Brooksdale. The other possibility is that Mary was a sister of Jim Green.

Folklore says Isobella was married one year after her parents went to Iowa. They then migrated in 1883 or possibly 1882.

Correction:
Embro West Zorra History Book - Historically Bound, Vol. 1, Page 773
Con 6, Lot 28 - Mrs. James Green's maiden name was Isabella Innes, daughter of Alexander Innes and Barbara McLean.

The Russel Innes Family of Lot 28, Con. 5
Front row: Russel Innes, Joyce Innes Smith, Jeannette Innes and Mary Innes McArthur
Back row: John Innes, Margaret Innes McLeod, Andrew Innes and Allan Innes

Cliff Kerr - Caretaker

Cliff Kerr who lived on Con. 4 Lot 29 is pictured with his wagon
which he took up and down the concession peddling his honey.
He was the caretaker at Wadland School SS #7 for many years.

ADAMS FAMILY
Lot 32 Con 9

The original house at Lot 32, con 9 was built in approximately 1830.
When a new house was built in 1888, the old house was moved to the edge of the barn and was used to keep pigs in.

Don & Gail Adams' grandsons, Samuel & Saywer Szmon are in front of a Massey-Harris tractor that has been used on the farm since 1960 (when it was bought used).

This picture of a car driving through the snow was taken in front of Adams Farm, Lot 32, Con 9 during the winter of 1939-1940

Don Adams standing in front of Wayne Smith's house, 1947.
Adams mail box is shown at the forefront - Lot 32, Con 10

PIONEER LAID TO REST

FUNERAL OF THE LATE RICHARD ADAMS, WELL KNOWN RESI-DENT OF E. NISSOURI AND ST. MARYS WAS LARGELY ATTEND-ED ON FRIDAY.

The funeral of the late Richard Adams, highly respected citizen of Queen Street East, and former pioneer farmer of the Ninth Concession, East Nissouri, who passed away so sudden-ly on Tuesday morning last, was held from the family residence on Friday afternoon and was largely attended, especially by his old neighbors of East Nissouri. The service of burial was conducted by Rev. A. B. Farney of St. James Anglican Church, the deceased having been a life long mem-ber of the Lakeside and St. Marys Anglican congregations, and the flow-er covered casket was borne to the grave by the following old and true friends of Mr. Adams: Honorary pall-bearers, Messrs. R. S. Box, John Pool, James Murray, Paul Bettridge, William Slater, William Smith. Pall-bearers, Robert Graham, W. H. Bartlett, Eli Day, A. J. Irvine, James Feightner, H. Gleason. Flower-bearers, Gordon Hut-ton, Victor Smith, Frederick, Ray and Glen Slater, H. D. Lang, John and Clifford Levy and Kenneth Hutton. Relatives from a distance who were present at the last sad rites, included, Mr. John and Miss Marilla Adams of Montreal, Mr. Freeman Adams and son Russell of Woodstock, Mr. and Mrs. James Robinson of Chatham and Dr. F. R. Slater of Hespeller. Mr. Adams, as all who knew him will testify, was a man of integrity, his word was as good as his bond and he was a true neighbor and a friend of all. He will be long remembered by the people of East Nissouri and the town of St. Marys.

The obituary of Richard Adams, grandfather of
Don Adams (Lot 32, Con 9)
Published in the St Marys newspaper 1932

ROBT. M'INTOSH, ANCHOR.   ROBT. M'LEOD.   E. L SUTHERLAND, CAPTAIN.   ALEX. CLARK.   WM. R. MUNRO.
IRA HUMMASON,

THE ZORRA TUG-OF-WAR TEAM.

Winners of the Cup and the Championship of America at the World's Fair Games at Chicago, August, 1893 —[Photo. by Hugill, Ingersoll, Ont.

Tug O War 1893 Chicago World's Fair Champs

CHICAGO WORLD'S FAIR TRIVIA

• Over 26 million people visited the 600 acre fairgrounds over 6 months

• The fair produced a number of firsts:
- Cream of Wheat - Juicy Fruit gum
- Pabst Blue Ribbon beer

• George Ferris Jr. tried to rival the Eiffel Tower (the highlight of the 1889 Paris fair) with his 264 foot tall wheel that could fit 2,150 people at one time. It cost 50¢ to ride (twice the price of a ticket to the fair).

Zorra Fuzion Bantam B 2014 Regular Season Champs 2014 LLFHL League Champs

After placing first overall in the Central West Division for regular season play, the Bantam B team travelled to Mississauga, Ontario on the weekend of March 28-30, 2014 to participate in the LLFHL Championship weekend. They played against teams from Lindsay, Vaughan and Blyth/Brussels. The Gold game was against Vaughan where they won 2-0. As you can see, this team consists of only 12 skaters and 1 goalie. These girls come from Embro, Thamesford, Harrietsville, St Marys, Kintore, and Woodstock. Team work, hard work, perseverance and sportsmanship is something this team proved every time they took to the ice.

Coaching staff: L-R Jayne Whetstone Trainer, Mark Bates Defense Door Coordinator, Jeff Irwin Assistant Coach, Rob Oliver Head Coach
Players back row L-R: Morgan Thomson (Staff), Mackie Winter, Brynn Oliver, Alison McKay, Abby Luther, Lindsay Bessegato, Grace McLeod
Front row L-R: Belle de Graaf, Brook Annett, Kate Irwin, Kyra Prekup, Katie Whetstone, Reese Gartly, Megan Bates

Helping the United Way

Township staff raise funds for United Way 2014

Township of Zorra Memorial Trees

Memorial tree signs including name plaques have been erected in the Grace Patterson Park, Thamesford, Embro Pond and Harrington Conservation Area. Memorial trees can be purchased at the township office for $40 through the Upper Thames River Conservation Authority (UTRCA). Have your loved ones name added to a sign or all three signs when you purchase a tree for an additional fee per name plaque.

The Township of Zorra hosted an unveiling event for the new Memorial Tree Signs on July 10, 2015. All names were added to the sign of those honoured through the program since it began in 1995.

Zorra Memorial Forest

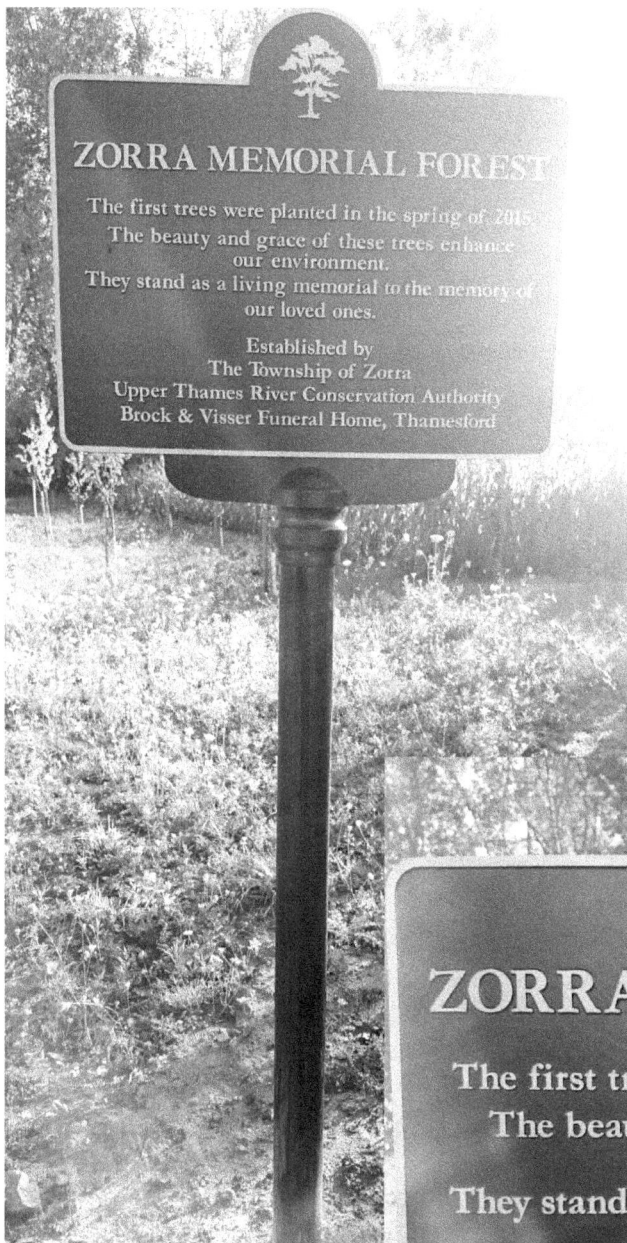

Memorial Forest created in partnership with
Brock and Visser Funeral Home
Thamesford Chapel
and UTRCA.
The forest is located on the 43rd Line,
north of Hwy 2.

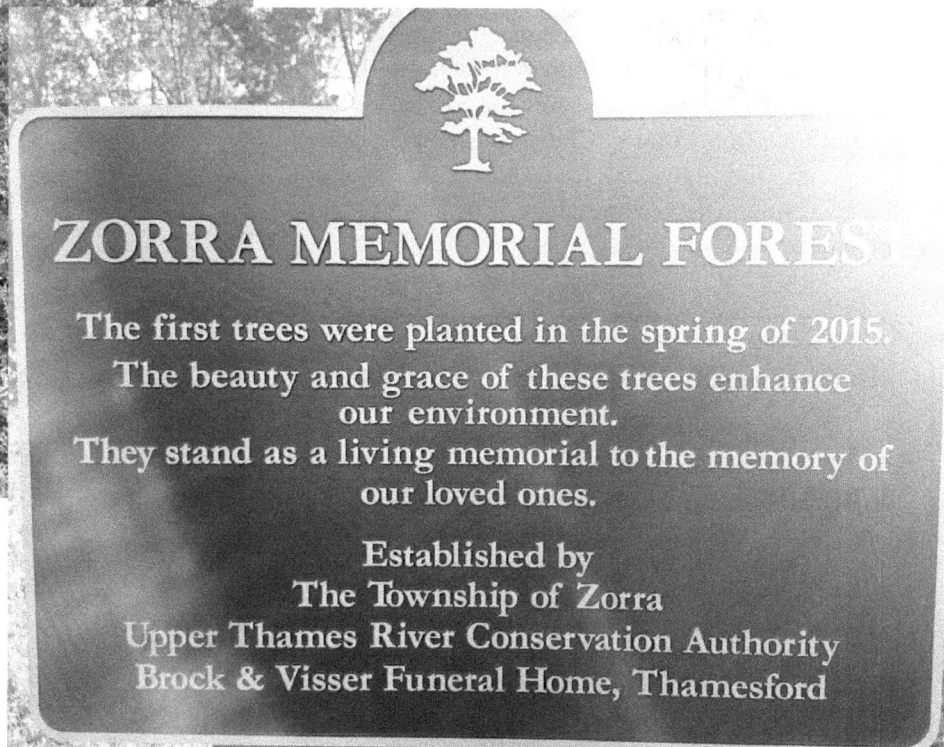

ZORRA MEMORIAL FOREST

The first trees were planted in the spring of 2015.
The beauty and grace of these trees enhance
our environment.
They stand as a living memorial to the memory of
our loved ones.

Established by
The Township of Zorra
Upper Thames River Conservation Authority
Brock & Visser Funeral Home, Thamesford

2014 Senior of the Year

The Senior of the Year award is presented to an individual who, after age 65, has enriched the social or civic life of their community without thought of personal or financial gain. Chris Cockle was presented with the Senior of the Year 2014 award from Mayor Margaret Lupton, for his outstanding volunteering throughout the Township of Zorra. Chris Cockle accepts the Senior of the Year award and gives thanks for the recognition. Mr. Cockle notes "Life is finding your gift and success is sharing it with others."

2015 Senior of the Year

Zorra Council honoured Jack Broadfoot as the Senior of the Year 2015 for Zorra Township. Nominations for this award come from Council & are sent to the Ontario Ministry of Citizenship & Immigration. Jack spearheaded the campaign to buy a generator for Sakura House. Contributions from Lions' Clubs, businesses, other service groups and individuals have allowed the full cost of the generator to be covered along with a reserve for maintenance.

Another reason for Jack to celebrate in 2015...

BROADFOOT 50th ANNIVERSARY
Jack & Julia Broadfoot, together with their family
invite you to join in celebrating their
Golden Wedding Anniversary
on August 1, 2015, from 2-4 pm
in the hall at Westminster United Church,
Thamesford.

Notice from the July 2015 Village Voice

Volunteer Appreciation Breakfast

In appreciation of our dedicated volunteers, the Township of Zorra hosted a Volunteer Appreciation Breakfast on October 2, 2015, 8:00am-10:00am. at the Embro-Zorra Community Centre.

The Township would like to recognize, celebrate and thank Zorra's many volunteers that we are so lucky to have in our community. One generous act can have a large impact on an entire community. Zorra Volunteers strengthen our community and improve quality of life.

North Oxford Township History Book

The North Oxford History Book Committee held their book launch on Sunday July 12, 2015 in the Beaty Room at the Thamesford Library.

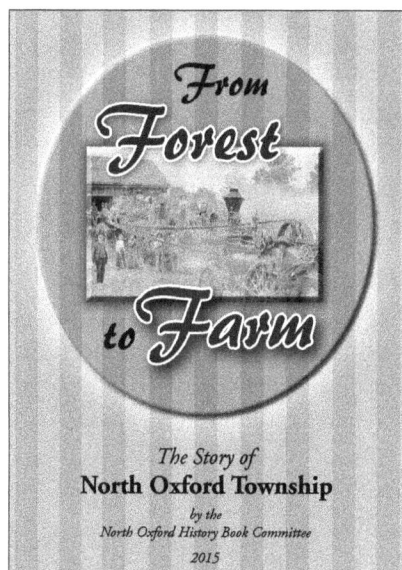

From Forest to Farm

The Story of
North Oxford Township
by the
North Oxford History Book Committee
2015

CO Alarm Law Comes into Effect

Left to right: Paul Mitchell (Dist. Chief), Jim Manzer (Dist. Chief), Margaret Lupton (Mayor), Ernie Hardeman (MPP), John McFarlan (Fire Chief), Nelly Green (OFM), Bob Ross (Dist. Chief)

A Message from John Gignac

The Hawkins-Gignac Foundation is proud to see the final piece of Ontario's new CO alarm law be put into place – the law is officially enforceable as of April 15, 2015. Now CO alarms are mandatory across the province for every household at risk of CO, regardless of age. I'd like to remind Ontarians, that if you do not obey, you not only put your family in danger but you risk penalties. My family is comforted, knowing that Ontario citizens are now much less likely to experience a tragedy similar to what we have gone through.

This makes two Canadian jurisdictions (Ontario and Yukon) that have passed carbon monoxide alarm laws to ensure every citizen is protected. Our goal is to protect all Canadians. Visit www.endthesilence.ca website to view materials to help keep your family safe. This is highlighted by our new 'Get to Know CO' video series and a link to the Toronto Star production of 'The Time Has Come' video produced along with the Ontario Fire Marshal.

I was a firefighter for 34 years. But for close to seven years, I've had a new mission: to end the silence on The Silent Killer – carbon monoxide. My reasons are very personal. My niece Laurie Hawkins, her husband Richard and their two children Cassandra and Jordan all died from CO poisoning in December 2008. A blocked chimney vent forced carbon monoxide from their gas fireplace back into their home. To honour their memory, our charitable foundation promotes carbon monoxide education and raises funds to purchase CO alarms to be given to at-risk families by fire departments nationwide. My family's tragedy could have been prevented. They did not have a carbon monoxide alarm. Please, protect your family by installing CO alarms. Warn friends and relatives too. Don't let the silent killer take from your family, what it took from ours. And, if you are able, please donate to our cause. Together we can end the silence.

John Gignac, Co-Chair

New Rescue Device

By Laura Green

After reading his correspondence from DuPont Pioneer about Pioneer's new program called Funding Initiative for Rural Emergencies (FIRE), sales representative Ben Sterk, Sterk Seeds Ltd, approached Jim Manzer, District Chief/Thamesford Fire Station, to see if a "need" was there to fit the criteria. Pioneer is promoting safety in rural communities across Canada through donations to volunteer fire departments. Zorra Fire & Rescue Service decided to apply for funding for two grain entrapment rescue devices valued at $1,000 each. This device is used to aid first responders in the removal of a victim who has become entrapped in grain. Zorra Township is a mainly rural area with many on-farm storage facilities, so an additional two devices would enhance services. Thamesford and Uniondale Stations received the new devices. The Embro Station received one back in 2010 which was donated by Dennis Turvey, Highland Park Farms. These grain entrapment rescue devices were designed and manufactured by Lambton 4-H Farm Safety Club.

Standing with the new grain entrapment rescue device or also called the grain extrication tool by its designers/manufacturers the Lambton 4-H Farm Safety Club are Mayor Margaret Lupton, Marian and Ben Sterk, Sterk Seeds Ltd, sales representatives of DuPont Pioneer, John McFarlan, Fire Chief Zorra Fire & Rescue Service, Paul Mitchell District Chief/Uniondale Station and Jim Manzer/Thamesford Station. DuPont Pioneer donated a sum of $2,000 for the purchase of the two rescue devices through their Funding Initiative for Rural Emergencies (F.I.R.E.) program.

ROEDC
Rural Oxford Economic Development Corp.

Economic development services for Rural Oxford launched in January 2015. Armed with a strategic plan that outlined the economic priorities, the five rural townships joined together to address the issues and opportunities faced by local businesses.

The Rural Oxford Economic Development Corporation is a nonprofit organization, governed by a volunteer board of directors representing government, small business, and industry.

Bernia Wheaton, an award winning economic development specialist, heads up the day to day activities and programs that are designed to assist existing businesses, while simultaneously attracting new business and new workers to this prosperous region.

Bernia Wheaton

As a new entity, the board and staff joined together with the community to define and design a corporate identity. This branding process was led by 31st Line Strategic Communications, a local company with global experience in branding and marketing. This exercise led to the identification of five unique value points, that distinctly set Rural Oxford apart from every other rural community in Ontario. We can now say, that we are building strong, vibrant, caring communities where people and business can prosper.

Rural Oxford is the most prosperous community in Ontario.
It's easy to see why Rural Oxford's population is growing. Our natural resources are abundant. Agriculture, business and industry are thriving, innovative and diversified here, offering outstanding employment opportunities and contributing to excellent quality of life. This is reflected in our caring, affluent and culturally diverse communities.

Our enviable location gives Rural Oxford outstanding access to major routes and markets.

People and commerce are well connected within Rural Oxford and to the world. Our excellent road systems are in close proximity to ports, major airports, rail and US border crossings. The commercial, educational and healthcare facilities of major population centres are within easy driving distance. All of this is readily accessible, yet costs are lower here.

Our rural legacy has nurtured a generation of agricultural leaders.
Rural Oxford is well known for the leadership role it has played in Canadian agriculture. Tremendous crop diversity and value is evident in our fields, and innovation is one of the things we grow best. The county is known as the Dairy Capital of Canada for the quality of its cows, and its historic and vibrant milk and cheese industries.

Our caring community nurtures a healthy living and business environment.
Life is good in Rural Oxford. Our people look after each other with strong stewardship of our environment, food, recreation, tourism and culture. They freely volunteer their time for worthwhile community causes. The result is a healthy and safe environment where business and families thrive, whether they are new to the area or have lived here for generations.

We are defined by our people, our proximity, and our prosperity.
Working with the local design firm, Five Point Design, the Rural Oxford EDC launched a website containing information about the organization, programs, and projects that are available to businesses in the community. This website celebrates our competitive advantage as a community, and is an information resource to every employer looking to enhance their business.

"Customer care" is a first priority for the ROEDC.
We are committed to helping people and businesses thrive in Rural Oxford. Our economic development professionals strive to do everything possible to mitigate barriers that could hinder good business growth in our communities. We do this in a positive, timely and confidential way.

Rural Oxford
Economic / Development

PEOPLE • PROXIMITY • PROSPERITY

In 2015, the ROEDC took on the following priorities.
To increase the awareness of the organization, and promote its programs and services.
To support professional development, workshops and training opportunities for the existing workforce.
To decrease retail leakage by encouraging local shopping. Enhance workforce development and employment opportunities for adults and youth.
The following is a little bit of information about how these priorities were addressed by staff at the ROEDC. Perhaps you have seen the Rural Oxford EDC logo popping up around your community. Parades, signs, brochures, and other marketing activities have been initiated to raise the awareness of the organization, and the services that it provides to local business. 'Life is Good' in rural Oxford, but we must continue to work toward future growth and opportunity.

The Business Builders workshop series is a collaboration amongst local business associations to bring a series of professional development seminars into rural Oxford. With the half-day conference kicking off in September, over 120 businesses gathered together to learn about opportunities for online marketing, email marketing, and social media communications to benefit small business. Since that launch, dozens of workshops have taken place in Tillsonburg, Ingersoll, Woodstock, Norwich, and Tavistock. With local experts delivering tips and tactics to help small businesses reach their audience. These workshops have been very well received, and will continue into 2016.

Technical training for the manufacturing and industrial sector has also been organized and launched in 2015. Relevant courses have been delivered in the community, to ensure that our workforce is as competitive and highly skilled as it can be. In December, courses in Working At Heights, have been brought to high school students who are on a career path to go directly to the workforce upon graduation. By partnering with school boards and teachers, youth now have the opportunity to show their future employer that they're serious about working in rural Oxford. Customized training and collaborative certifications will continue into 2016. Employers can also tap into the Canada-Ontario Jobs Grant, which subsidizes training that is in demand by our agricultural, construction, and manufacturing industries.

Reducing retail leakage, by encouraging people to shop locally, is no easy task. The statistics show that well over 3,000 people travel every day from rural Oxford for employment outside of their home township. This often leads to shopping in large urban centers, rather than supporting home town merchants. With this in mind, the Buy Close By program was designed and implemented in 2015. Introduced in Norwich township, the ROEDC partnered with the Business Improvement Association, the Chamber of Commerce, and merchants in an effort to remind people how critically important it is to buy close by. This innovative program caught the attention of Wei Chen at CBC radio, who invited Bernia Wheaton onto Ontario Mornings for an interview to discuss this creative approach to local shopping. This program, that rewards those who buy close by, will be extended to all five rural townships in 2016.

The assembly of a business directory is now in the works. With almost 5,000 businesses in Rural Oxford, staff are gathering names and contact information to develop a robust database of information that will be a resource to all businesses and community groups.

It's been a busy inaugural year for the ROEDC. The foundation has been laid for 2016 where work will continue as we build a strong and robust rural economy.

Oxford People Against the Landfill

Stop the Dump! A Brief History

While it may seem like a lot longer ago, it was in fact in March 2012 that our community heard about Walker's intention to put a dump into an active quarry near the Thames River, the Quarry Lake, private and municipal wells on a property spanning Zorra and Southwest Oxford and close to Ingersoll.

Jeremy Richardson and Ben Lampkin wasted no time in calling a public meeting which resulted in the formation of OPAL, Oxford People Against the Landfill, and the decision to rally in a park. Hundreds then headed up past the historic cemetery to look at the quarry that Carmeuse is said to plan to lease to Walker. They gazed at the pristine waters of the Quarry Lake, the Thames River and the scenic Beachville Road.

Walker begins the Terms of Reference. Convinced that local municipal councils need to be informed about the regulations regarding pits and quarries' rehabilitation and previous decisions by the Ontario Municipal Board regarding land use, Steve McSwiggan, founding president of OPAL, Suzanne Crellin, then of OPAL, now president of OEAC; Mike Farlow, a Community Liaison Committee member; Reed Elliott, a local expert in the Aggregate Resources Act; Bryan Smith, chair of the Oxford Coalition for Social Justice, and others, tour the municipalities and county councils multiple times. Simultaneously, OPAL and allied groups begin letter-signing extravaganzas which, in 18 months, net over 12,000 letters from local residents and sympathetic Ontarians asking the Minister of the Environment to say "No" to the dump. By late November 2015, the letter total reached 45,720 not counting emails and phone calls to the Ministry of the Environment.

Ministry officials critique the Terms of Reference and call for Walker to revise it. Independent scientists for OPAL and the Oxford Coalition for Social Justice denounce Walker's proposal on scientific grounds. The Ministry grants a time-out to Walker in both March and November of 2014 to fix their proposal. OPAL retains the Canadian Environmental Law Association to advise. Help that becomes necessary when later in June 2015, the MOE secretively allows the dumping of industrial sewage into the Quarry Lake after a consultation period ending on Christmas Day 2014, when the public's thoughts might be on other things. Nonetheless, local newspapers declare the dump the story of the year!

The OPAL Alliance stages multiple information sessions for the public, inviting world-renowned water warrior Maude Barlow, Charlie Angus and John Vanthof to speak of winning the Adams Mine dump fight, George Henry and Chief R.K. Joe Miskokomon of the Chippewas of the Thames on their inalienable rights to clean water to drink and to catch fish. Though invited, Glen Murray, Minister of the Environment does not attend, does not send a representative, or write a statement to be read at the event.

Then, in September, 2015, it was time for 'Queen's Park with Cows', an event where two bovine beauties and sundry Oxfordians visited a session of the Legislature. No, they wouldn't let the cows inside or make speeches in front of the Legislature. No, the cows didn't do that, or any other expected thing on the lawn. An invite to Mr. Murray was extended for him to come to the microphone. He was not there!

October comes and goes. A federal government changes and the new PM appoints an Ontarian to a new job, Minister of the Environment and Climate Change, the same title as Glen Murray has. OPAL sends her mail too in hopes that a new Canadian government will want to use the laws available to protect human and environmental health. On the provincial front, we still wait for Mr.

Glen Murray to make a decision on the very first step of a very long process, a process made longer by the time-outs accorded Walker and the time for Mr. Murray's staff to read the reams of letters which change often but say "Stop the dump" for many reasons and from many people. We await a decision.

Ruling on Zorra Gravel Pits

The Council of the Township of Zorra passed an Interim Control By-law to place a moratorium on new or expanded gravel pits and stone quarries for a one-year period in the Township of Zorra located south of Rd 74. The by-law will prohibit the Township from processing any new zone change applications, new or expanded gravel pits, or stone quarries while a policy review is carried out on the current mineral extraction provisions in the Oxford County Official Plan. This section of the Official Plan considers policies and review criteria to be applied to proposals for new or expanded quarry and sand and gravel licenses. This includes ensuring compatibility with the natural environment, settlement areas and agriculture. Township Council has taken the step of passing an interim control by-law after experiencing frustration with the lack of coordination and management of aggregate extraction through the approval regulator, Ontario Ministry of Natural Resources and Forestry.

A recent provincial review of the Aggregate Resources Act failed to address how the government would assess the cumulative effects of noise, dust, truck traffic and the overall social economic issues of impacts of concentrating multiple aggregate operations in a small geographic area like those found in aggregate rich regions of Zorra Township. The Township of Zorra is home to 48 licensed sand, gravel and quarry operations that cumulatively cover approximately 2,730.95 ha (6,748.08 ac) of land. Taken together, these 48 licensed operations are approved for a maximum annual extraction of over 25.4 million tonnes of material. For comparison, this area would cover over 27% of the area of the Town of Richmond Hill and over 10% of the City of Mississauga. The policy review study is expected to be completed within a one-year time frame as permitted in the Planning Act. The study time frame may be extended for an additional year if needed to complete a more thorough review.

"The Township recognizes the significant role the aggregate industry has played in Zorra's development. However, Council's priority is to put into place a review process that takes into account the various impacts on citizens that live in close proximity to multiple aggregate operations. We realize that Zorra is an aggregate rich municipality; however, our citizens have placed their trust in us when it comes to protecting their health and well being, and we are obligated to act in their best interests," said Margaret Lupton, Mayor of Zorra Township.

"The Township has been lobbying the government since 2006 to put a process in place that takes into account the cumulative impacts. We had hoped the review of the Aggregate Resources Act would have done so. It is our position that valid concerns raised by Council were ignored, which left the Township no choice but to carry out its own review that aims for more stringent development standards," said Ron Forbes, Deputy Mayor of Zorra Township.

Dutch-Canadian
Friendship Tulip Garden

On Wednesday, October 28, 2015 a public ceremony was held at the cenotaph in front of the Township of Zorra office. Through a grant program, the township was the recipient of 500 tulip bulbs. This grant was made possible due to the generous partnership of the Canadian Garden Council, Vesey's Bulbs, Canada Post, Canadian Tulip Festival, National Capital Commission, Canadian Nursery Landscape Association, Garden Making Magazine, Chimpanzee, Baxter Travel Media, Enterprise Canada, Gardens BC, Quebec Gardens' Association and the Ontario Garden Tourism Coalition.

The Dutch-Canadian Friendship Tulip Garden was planted at the cenotaph which is in front of the Zorra Township Office. The public was welcome to attend this event and was encouraged to bring with them any friends or family members who were veterans.

The garden acts as a colourful reminder of the sacrifices Canadians and our own Heroes of Zorra have given over the years. The Township of Zorra is honoured to be chosen as one of the 140 Canadian communities that received a tulip garden.

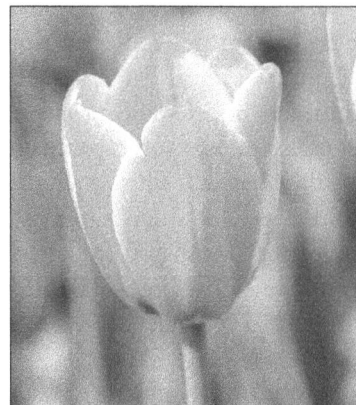

From the fall of 1944 to the spring of 1945, the First Canadian Army played a major role in liberating the Netherlands from Nazi occupation.

During this operation, more than 7,600 Canadians lost their lives.

Their sacrifice and their part in freeing the population from hunger and hardship earned for Canadian soldiers the lasting gratitude of the Dutch people. A warm friendship still exists between the two countries.

To commemorate the 70th anniversary of the Liberation of the Netherlands, the Government of Canada and surviving veterans will take part in commemorative events in the Netherlands from May 3–9, 2015.

DUTCH CANADIAN HISTORY

from www.veterans.gc.ca

The liberation of the Netherlands, played a key role in the culmination of the Second World War, as the Allied forces closed in on Germany from all sides. The Dutch people had suffered terrible hunger and hardship under the increasingly desperate German occupiers.

Big Brothers Big Sisters
40th Anniversary

Former and current members (volunteers, children and their families) attended a special 40th Anniversary Reunion Saturday, June 20, 2015 at the Elm Hurst Inn Carriage House in Ingersoll. The event included historical memorabilia and photos, a time capsule, refreshments, and renewal of friendships and speeches from past volunteers, littles and community members. Over the past 40 years, the agency has impacted the lives of over 1,700 children through their mentoring programs and services! Today Big Brothers Big Sisters of Ingersoll, Tillsonburg & Area provides 12 mentoring programs to fit everyone's lifestyle and time commitment.

The local Big Brother chapter in Ingersoll was incorporated in February 1975 with Big Sisters forming in 1982. In 1986 both agencies amalgamated to create Ingersoll & District Big Brothers Big Sisters. Through conversations and an agreement with Big Brothers Big Sisters of Tillsonburg & District, Ingersoll & District Big Brothers Big Sisters expanded their service delivery area to include the community of Tillsonburg and surrounding area; adjusting their by-laws accordingly. The Tillsonburg agency was a vital agency for many years before they closed their doors in January 2001. In October 2001, the agency was renamed Big Brothers Big Sisters of Ingersoll, Tillsonburg & Area Inc.

Three funds have been introduced over the years – Berdine Hurley Bursary (providing financial assistance to Little Brothers and Little Sisters attending a post-secondary institution or trade school - $23,000 to 32 recipients since 1993!); Ryan Landon Memorial Fund (to fund agency activities or resources benefiting several children in the program and an award to recognize a former or current youth member who has overcome obstacles); and the Mary Smith Memorial Fund (to provide funding for annual Children's Christmas Party and an award to honour and recognize an agency volunteer who has gone "above and beyond").

Even though it's been 40 years of mentoring relationships our current children's needs for mentorship and support are still great. Today's youth face greater challenges than before. We are committed to continuing to provide them with quality mentoring relationships to help them reach their potential. Each year we service over 240 children in the community through various programs but not all have a BIG to call on. Help us bring in 2016 strong and start the next 40 years with a flock of support for our community's youth and families.

Big Brothers Big Sisters
40th Anniversary

Big Brothers Big Sisters
40th Anniversary

Municipal Election
Monday, October 27, 2014

Your 2014 - 2018 Council

Our Mayor
Margaret Lupton

Ward One Councillor
Ron Forbes

Ward Two Councillor
Marie Keasey

Ward Three Councillor
Marcus Ryan

Ward Four Councillor
Doug Matheson

Reflections of Yesteryear

The Family Farm Woodlot

By Jim Verwer

Spring is the best time of year to look for spots in the bush where maple syrup was made generations ago. They are getting more difficult to find each year, covered by leaves and fallen branches, invisible to the untrained eye - yet evidence of the fire pits used to boil down sap can still be found today in most farm woodlots. Cracked and blackened from the heat of fires that have long since died out. Stones where iron bars were laid across to support the sap pan testify to the annual spring event held on the family farm generations ago. Stories and memories still abound from those able to recall tapping tress and how everyone on the farm contributed to the task which not only provided a staple food for the kitchen table but also assisted with grocery money for the upcoming year.

Often the names of the folks who once helped with the undertaking can be found on the beech trees nearby and testify to their authors who worked under the forest canopy years ago. Young and old alike carved their names on them, often along a path used to haul out firewood or on a tree close to their favourite fishing spot if there happened to be a stream.

These are the remainders of those who not only laboured there but those who came to enjoy nature. Those were the days when children would break the long hours of farm work and escape to a place of refuge and seize the moment by inscribing the date and their initials on a living memorial.

There once was a time when the whole family would walk back to the bush on a beautiful Sunday afternoon, often accompanied by visitors or guests, and leave their names behind to create that era's social media. We had our own "Family Tree" beside Cole Creek that everyone left their mark on, and over the years it became cluttered and included the signatures of overseas relatives and the year they visited.

Evidence from long-gone families from the former Township of East Nissouri can be discovered on the beech trees along Cole Creek. Signs of unknown writers from the last century stare back at you when you go for a walk in an farm woodlot. But as the trees succumb to time, and the distractions of modern life divert our attention from them, they will become increasingly more difficult to find, and eventually disappear, along with the spot in the bush where maple syrup was once made.

EMBRO

Embro Mill 1909

Embro Ball Diamond Improvements

New lights, new fencing for Embro's Ball Diamond

By Laura Green

Ball players will no longer depend on the moonlight to see the long distant balls thanks to a $36,000 grant from the Ontario Trillium Foundation and the support of the local businesses of Highland Fence, D & D Electric, Dufferin Concrete and D & J Paton Bros. Embro Minor Ball installed two light standards in the back field and a home run fence covered with white tile plastic at the ball diamond at Matheson Park in Embro. Embro Minor Ball thanked the Lakeside Grinders and Embro Slow Pitch for their labour. Chair, John Chalkley, in his thank you, stated, "Your investment in our ball park is an investment in the youth of our community."

Standing in the infield on July 24 with the new fence and lighting in the background are members of Embro Minor Ball Linda Heather, Jeff Heather, John Chalkley, Oxford M.P.P. Ernie Hardeman, Kathy O'Neil and Colleen Belore Photo by Laura Green

Embro Lawn Bowling Improvements

Embro Lawn Bowling Club received a Trillium grant for $31,000, allowing them to do a major renovation to their club house including installing handicap access to the facility and a beautiful handicap washroom. They also added a beautiful new kitchen, laminate flooring and new tables and chairs. The existing washrooms received a total make over as well.

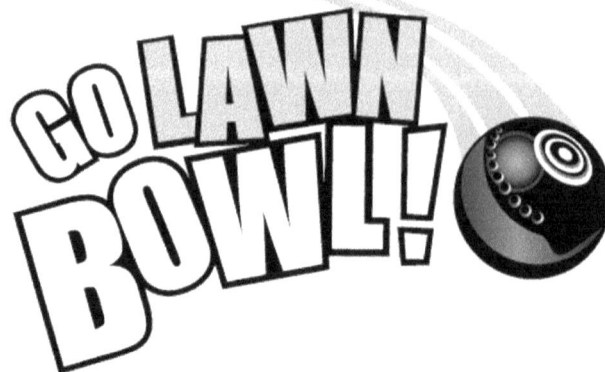

St. Andrew's Day Celebrated

Honouring the Patron Saint of Scotland
...by the Scots and want to be Scots in Embro
By Laura Green

In Scotland, and many countries with Scottish connections, St Andrew's Day is marked with a celebration of Scottish culture including traditional Scottish food, music and dancing. Zorra Caledonian Society President Steve MacDonald used the Gaelic expression "Cead Mile Failte" to begin his opening remarks for the 79th Annual St. Andrew's Night Banquet held on November 27, 2015 at the Embro Community Centre. Haggis, Tatties and Neeps were part of the roast turkey dinner prepared and served by Janice's Fine Country Catering, Uniondale. "God Save the Queen" and "O Canada" was lead by Ruth Ross. Grace was said by Past President Jamie McPherson. Entertainment was provided by the Ingersoll Pipe Band, Sim School of Highland Dance, Celtic music by Dan MacDonald (fiddle) and Jacob McCauley (bodhran) and a Snapshot of Scotland by Ron and Wendy Marshall who organized a tour of Scotland for the Zorra Caledonia Society in the summer of 2015.

One important tradition of this Scottish Meal is the address to the Haggis. Jennifer Moodie recited Robbie Burns "Address to the Haggis" and 1st Vice president Geoff Innes was the Haggis Bearer. Standing on guard is President Steve MacDonald and secretary Warren McKay. The evening ended with the singing of "Auld Lang Syne".

Three generations of the Thomson family of Embro celebrated their Scottish heritage at the 78th Annual St. Andrew's Night Banquet on November 28, 2014 at the Embro Community Centre. Both father (Tom) and son (Angus) are past presidents of the Zorra Caledonian Society. Tom and his wife Margaret emigrated to Canada with their two sons Angus and Alan and purchased a dairy farm in the Curries area. In 1974, they changed their careers, they purchased the car dealership from Reuben Brenneman in Embro and their third son Tommy was born in 1975. Angus's daughter Carlan is a first generation

Jennifer Moodie recites the 'Address to Hagis' as Hagis Bearer, Geoff Innes holds the dish

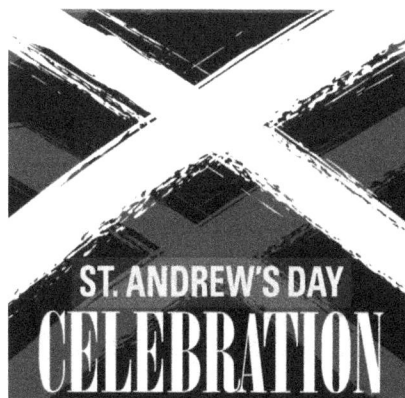

37

Embro Fair 2014

The following was printed in The Village Voice

EXCITING NEW THINGS AT THE FAIR

The weekend will kick off with the ambassador competition on Friday evening at 7pm. This evening there will be a Family Feud competition (just like the popular game show). New at the fair this year is Zip Lining, Let's Talk Science & wood carving demonstrations. This year we will have a silent auction throughout the weekend. There is also the return of many favourites such as the dairy show, horse show, talent show, tug o war, pet show & baby show. There are rides and many activities for kids of all ages. A special effort has been made to have fun things for older kids. This year we have a new band at our large Saturday Night 19+ Dance. Kerosene Creek is the band featured at this year's Fair.

38

Embro Fair 2015

MacKay is Embro Fair Ambassador

By Laura Green

"You ladies were incredible" was the opening comment of the judge, Linda Slits, 2012 CNE Ambassador, who spoke on behalf of the other two judges, Adrianna Van Oostveen, Coordinator, Programming and Events 4-H Ontario and Paul MacLeod, Past President of Holstein Canada. Katelyn MacKay, who was sponsored by Oxford Feed & Supply, and Jillian Ross, who was sponsored by Braemar Women's Institute, were interviewed by the judges, had supper with them and presented their prepared and impromptu speeches to a large audience of fans and fair supporters at the opening night of the Embro Fall Fair held at the Embro Community Centre Sept 18.

While the judges deliberated for an hour, the audience was entertained by the game "Are you Smarter than a 4-Her." 4-H members of the 100th Anniversary Club challenged past 4-H members Ruud Arts, Doug Matheson, Julie McIntosh and Shonna Ward. When the final points were totalled, the past 4-H members came out on top.

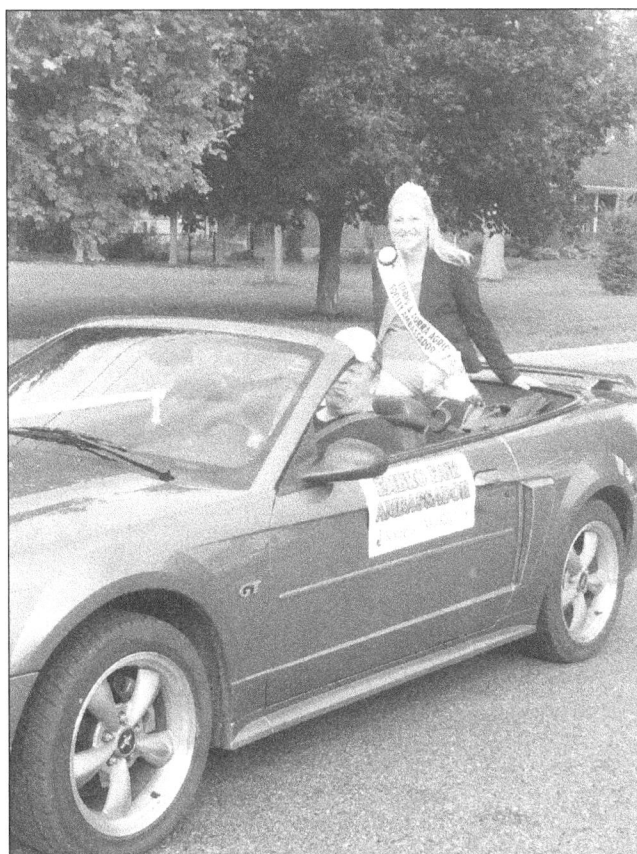

Community Service Award winner for 2015, Julie McIntosh, officially opened the 157th Embro Fall Fair. Jenna Chalkley, 2014-2015 Ambassador, gave her touching farewell speech. Then new 2015-16 Embro Fair Ambassador was introduced. Katelyn MacKay is a 2015 University of Guelph graduate with a Bachelor of Science in Agriculture with a major in Animal Science. She is working as a ruminant formulator at Shur-Gain in St. Marys.

The Embro Fall Fair theme was the highlight of the year for the Embro & Zorra Agricultural Society, since it was "Explore 4-H, Celebrating 100 years of 4-H in Ontario". Members of the 100th Anniversary project were wearing the green shirts they designed especially for this year as they accompanied the sign and showed some of the variety of great projects available. The Celebration Dinner at the Embro & Zorra Community Centre on Sat, Sept 19, started with a group photo at 5:30. Dinner was catered by Belmont Town Catering.

Wienerfest Home County Festival

Helping Homeless pets and celebrating all that is dachshund is the idea behind Wienerfest.

Wienerfest Home County Festival is Canada's largest breed specific event, focused on Dachshunds. In 2013, over 6,000 people and 1,000 dogs attended.

It's a free family and dog friendly daylong event, that provides funding for pet rescue and raises awareness for the plight of abandoned and abused animals in Canada.

There are many fun events, such as the ever popular Dachshund Races, as well as costume contests, and professional photo opportunities with the "wienermobile". Over 100 exhibitors have booths, selling products such as animal dietary products, clothing, leashes, pet services and personal handicrafts. Numerous local and nationally recognized businesses, who are sponsors, also attend. Visitors can choose from a wide variety of food services from local charities and food trucks.

A veterinarian and a pet trainer are onsite all day, to answer questions visitors may have regarding their pets.

All well-mannered dogs of all breeds are welcome and will be considered "honourary" dachshunds for the day. Animals must be on a leash at all times. Flexi leashes are not allowed.

Wienerfest Home County Festival operates under the umbrella of Tiny Paws Dog Rescue, a registered Canadian Charity (Business Number 82942 3920 RR0001).

Tiny Paws Dog Rescue works with shelters, pounds, other rescues and private individuals to save dogs that might otherwise be euthanized and places those dogs into private foster homes. They provide standard veterinary care and other needed medical treatment, work on training issues and through their adoption screening process, find new forever homes for the dogs in their care. Tiny Paws also educates the public about the important reasons to spay/neuter pets, the deplorable conditions found in puppy mills, the sources of pet store dogs and the need to adequately care for and train the family pet. An estimated two million dogs enter Canadian shelters and rescue organizations each year: close to one million are euthanized. Tiny Paws strives hard, every day, every week to reduce that number.

Wienerfest 2015

Embro Teen to be a National Paddler

By Laura Green

Sitting on the back deck of her Embro home, a bubbly teen was having a difficult time containing her enthusiasm about the next two important weeks of her dragon boat racing career. Thirteen-year-old, Marleena Coull, will be the youngest member of Canada's National Junior Dragon Boat team to compete at the World Championships. The grade 9 student will travel to Welland Ontario to compete with her team on August 19-23, 2015 at the Welland International Flatwater Centre. It is predicted to have approximately 4,000 accredited individuals in attendance from 30 plus countries.

The Canadian athletes are defending the 2013 World Dragon Boat Racing Champion title that was won after winning 30 races at the championship held in Szeged, Hungary.

Coull's interest in the sport began back in 2012 after a presentation at her school by the Woodstock Dragon Boat Racing Club. Coull joined her school's (Ste. Marguerite Bourgeoys) recreational team and began to enjoy the sport. In the spring of 2013, Coull heard about a travelling team, the South Western Ontario Dragon

Boat racing club who were heading to Orlando Florida and Disney World to compete in October. Winning races there caused Coull to catch the racing fever.

For the past two seasons, Coull has been practicing twice a week with the Stratford Dragon Boat club. The club started preparing interested members who wanted to try-out for the national teams back in the fall of 2014. The early start paid off for seven members of the Stratford Club who will represent Team Canada at the Worlds. Try-outs included training camps, fitness testing, paddling tests and a selection camp held in May. For western Canada the try-outs were held in Vancouver and for Eastern Canada it was held in Toronto. Twenty-four boys and twenty-four girls were chosen from the two camps and will practice as a team from August 11-18 at the National Team training camp at Niagara College's Niagara on the Lake campus.

Another National Junior team member is Megan Finnessy from Woodstock. Coull also practices once a week with the Thames River Paddling Club at Wildwood Conservation Area. Her other summer time sport is soccer with the Embro U15 team and in the winter she uses her talents skating with the Zorra Skating Club.

41

Cambrocourt Manor in Embro Celebrates 25 Years

The Optimist Creed contains a powerful message for all of us. One which is very hard to attain. It represents the ultimate in club fellowship and the highest degrees of perfection to which human nature is capable of attaining. It is needs and demands of a community which lights the flame in all service clubs. Embro West Zorra Optimist Club accepted these challenges through club meetings, ideas, organized community meetings and yes, lively discussions on the odd occasion, the club was able to raise the roof in the construction of Cambrocourt Manor.

Today Embro and Area Seniors Housing is a non-profit corporation run by a volunteer Board of Directors and one staff member. The Corporation's mandate is to provide moderate cost housing for senior citizens. Rental assistance is available for tenants who qualify. Our building consists of 18 one bedroom units, five two bedroom units and one handicap suite. It has made it possible for many seniors to be able to live independently in a beautiful rural community.

In October of 1986 the Optimists decided it would be worthwhile to investigate the construction of an apartment complex for seniors. Robert Berge, secretary for the board of directors for this project, says the incentive came from the idea of keeping people in their own community. Al Matheson, a club member and past president of the

Embro Optimist Club said, "We thought it made sense with Canada's population aging. We've always been concerned with the problem which faces our local people. Once they get to the point where they're no longer able to look after their homes, they have to move out of the area. We arrived at this as a way of keeping seniors in their own community." The board approached those responsible for the senior's residence at nearby Innerkip for advice and after that meeting decided to survey the community and hire a consulting firm.

The results of a questionnaire, sent out to the community residents, were positive. The consulting firm, Gibson and Associates, from Toronto, handled the paperwork for the joint funding from the province through Ontario Housing and federal government via Canada Mortgage and Housing Corporation.

The committee located five acres of property fronting on Oxford County Road 6, on the southern limits of the village of Embro. A public meeting was held at the community centre to explain the development that was taking place in the area. Funding of the project was obtained in the fall of 1987 and final plans worked out. The 24 unit apartment complex was designed by Brian Smith an architect with Robert Reimers Architects, Toronto. Construction started in the summer of 1988 by Cogent Construction from Hyde Park.

The Optimists wanted a building that would blend in well with the surrounding countryside and the village's architecture. "This particular group was very much involved with the preliminary designs," said Smith. "We get a better product when they make us work so hard. Their input shows their strong commitment." Smith adapted the "domestic features of an Ontario farm house" into the design. A wide porch, gables, large windows and brick exterior help to create a two story building that's in keeping with the context of the community. A

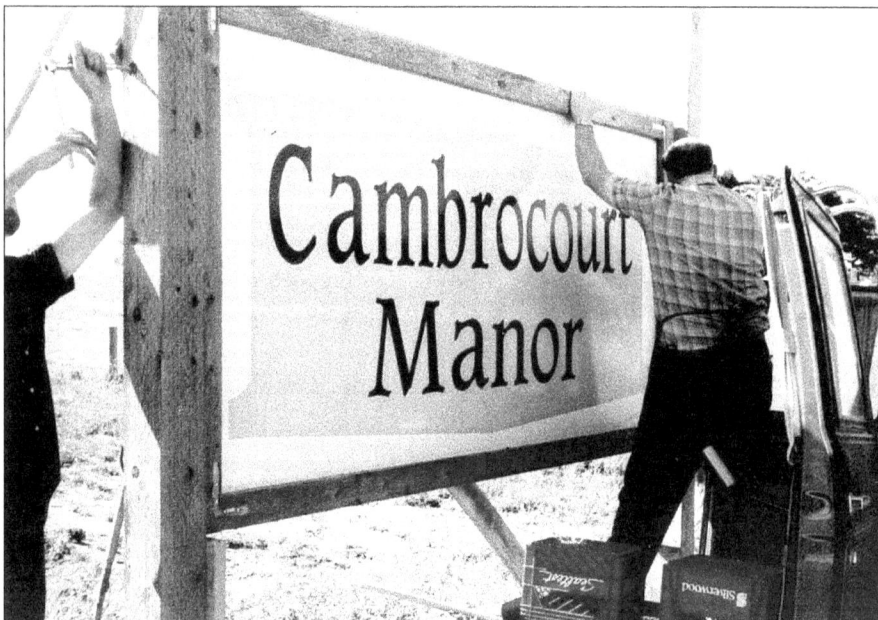

tower was added to disguise the elevator. Purchase of Part of Lot 11 Concession 4, Township of Zorra, consisting of five acres from Mr. Charles A. Campbell was made in March of 1988 for $40,000.

On April 6, 1988 Optimist Club of Embro and Zorra President, Brian McCowan and Secretary, Scott Berge, officially sold their interest of Cambrocourt Manor from the Optimist Club to the newly formed corporation Embro and Area Seniors Housing Corporation for the sum of $1.00.

The original Board of Directors were Chairperson James Verhoef, Allan Matheson, Robert Berge, Robert McRoberts, James Stricklar, Ross Smith, Wayne MacKinnon, Lester Shelly, Brian McCowan, Tom Thomson, William Murray and Richard Leonhardt.

Members of the Optimist Club consciously worked hard at maintaining a sense of community within the building itself. This beautiful facility is located in the highlands of Embro and has many features including a beautiful panoramic country view, secure entrance, bathroom safety bars, on site laundry facilities, hairdressing facilities, library, games room and a beautiful relaxing lounge.

The official opening ceremony of the building was held at an Open House on September 15, 1989.

Many names were proposed for the building during a contest. Some of the names included Highland Haven, Embro Heights, Valley View, Hillside View, Zorra Manor, Highland Heights, The House on the Hill and Embro Villa. The winning entry was submitted Dorothy Day with the name Cambrocourt Manor.

The building is 23,529 sq feet. One bedroom apartments are approximately 600 sq ft. and two bedroom apartments are 800 sq ft.

Many individuals, organizations and business took great interest in the project and made wonderful donations of time and gifts for the building. Gifts such as a piano for

the lounge, paintings, plants, games, furniture and many other things were added to enhance the comfort and feeling of home for the 29 original tenants. Even the local school children became involved with the donation of two flowering trees from Zorra Highland Park Public School. School buses stopped at the complex before school one Monday morning and the children participating in the presentation and planting of two flowering crab trees.

Martha Andrews started her job as Administrator on April 27, 1989

The first tenant was Mr. Ted Woch on May 20, 1989.

As time goes on:
Cambrocourt Manor continues to provide moderately priced housing to seniors citizens and is still run by a Board of Directors and one staff member.
Administrators of Cambrocourt Manor have included:
Mrs. Martha Andrews 1989 - 1995
Mrs. Carol Verhoef 1995
Mrs. Mary Beck 1995-97
Mrs. Lynne Heersink 1997 to present.

In March of 2006 original tenants, Mr. and Mrs. Frank Cottrill, Laura Ford, Ted Woch, and Joanne (Moleanar) Snider still resided at Cambrocourt.

The 10 year anniversary, September 26, 1999, was celebrated by planting a red maple tree on the north side of the building and by having an open house.

Cambrocourt Manor continues to be a vibrant part of the community with approximately 100 people who have called Cambrocourt Manor their home. We have had three marriages performed in the lounge. Various groups have entertained us including: Junior Farmers games nights, piano recitals, Girl Guide and Boy Scout functions, school functions i.e. Valentine Tea's, Country Jamboree's, pot lucks, Christmas turkey dinners, Mother Goose, and Oxford Community Child Care.

Cambrocourt Manor continues to change with the addition of a gas fireplace in the lounge in 2004 and new furniture in the lounge in 2003.

Many residents keep active in our community by doing volunteer work some of which include knitting sweaters for babies in Africa, sewing shopping bags for Africa, providing music for jamborees and cooking for seniors dinners at local churches.

It was party time at Cambrocourt Manor, Embro on October 4, 2014 to celebrate 25 years since the building officially opened on September 15, 1989. Seating on the chairs are the two longest residents – Grace Barons (1990) & Joanne Snider (1989). In the second row is current administrator, Lynne Heersink, first administrator, Martha Andrews (1989-1995), current board members of the Embro and Area Seniors Housing Corporation Diane Smith, Sharron Simmons and Marybel Brenneman. Back row is Corporation's charter board members James (Jim) Verhoef (1st chair), Lester Shelley and Robert McRoberts and past board member Dennis Weaver.

Optimist Creed

PROMISE YOURSELF

To be so strong that nothing can disturb your peace of mind

To talk health, happiness and prosperity to every person you meet

To make all your friends feel that there is something in them

To look at the sunny side of everything and make your optimism come true

To think only of the best to work only for the best and to expect only the best

To be just as enthusiastic about the success of others as you are about your own

To forget the mistakes of the past and press onto the greater achievements of the future

To wear a cheerful countenance at all times and give every living creature you meet a smile

To give so much time to the improvement of yourself that you have no time to criticize others

To be too large for worry, too noble for anger, too strong for fear,

and too happy to permit the presence of trouble

Optimist International

The Embro West Zorra Optimist Club accepted these challenges
and was able to raise the roof in the construction of Cambrocourt Manor.

Zorra Highland Park Graduation 2014

By Laura Green

The 2014 graduating class from Zorra Highland Park School had a special piper to pipe their class into the Embro Community Centre on June 25, 2014. Grade 8 student, Fraser Nagle who is member of the Ingersoll Pipe Band had the honors. Julia Bujouves, the school's new principal since January, welcomed guests & gave the opening remarks. Anita Fraser gave remarks from the Zorra Highland Park Parent Council / Home & School Association. Recognition Certificates were presented by Grade 8 Teachers Rob Thrasher & Greg Willows to the following students: Marisa Blewett, Cheyenne Chrysler, Isabel Cockle, Carly Donker, Grace Dow, Dane Eastman, Keelie Eaton, Marcus Frizelle, Madison Hall, Melissa Hough, Hannah Kirwin, Quinn Lee, Abby Luther, Kelly Maloney, Alexander McKay, Baily Monteith, Brett Munro, Fraser Nagle, Brynn Oliver, Kyra Prekup, Ashley Smith, Victoria Steinacker, Andrew Stoddart, Claire Van Dam, Emily Vleuten & Danielle Zilke. Honours certificates were also presented by the Grade 8 teachers.

Individual Subject Awards

Drama Award ....Isabel Cockle
Sponsored by Thistle Theatre

Jacqueline Witteveen Memorial Art Award ....
....Keelie Eaton

Music ....Hannah Kirwin

French ....Ashley Smith
Sponsored by Charles & Margaret Lupton

English ....Isabel Cockle
Sponsored by Brooksdale Women's Institute

Mathematics ....Brynn Oliver

Social Studies (History & Geography)....Melissa Hough
Sponsored by Allan & Ann Matheson

Health & Physical Education................Claire Van Dam
Sponsored by Elgie Bus Lines Ltd

Male Athlete of the Year................................Quinn Lee
Sponsored by Elgie Bus Lines Ltd

Female Athlete of the Year........................Hannah Zilke
Sponsored by Elgie Bus Lines Ltd

Science & Technology................................Fraser Nagle
Sponsored by Harrington & Area Community Association

Highest Academic......................................Isabel Cockle
Sponsored by Embro Cheese House

Citizenship ....Baily Monteith
Sponsored by Thistle Lodge No. 250

Perseverance Award ....Kyra Prekup
Sponsored by Zorra Caledonian Society

Jean Hossack Memorial Award ....Madison Hall

Katelynn Innes Memorial Award........Abby Luther, Arje
Sponsored by Rick & Margo Innes

Pelders Memorial Award..........................Kelly Maloney
Sponsored by Oxford Farm Safety

OPC – Principal's Award ....Fraser Nagle

Dr. Gordon Murray Scholarships ....Isabel Cockle
....Grace Dow & Fraser Nagle

On behalf of the Western Ontario Drama League, Harold Arbuckle, Chris Cockle & Abby Cockle presented Adjudicators Special Award to the Tech Crew from Theatre Theatre's production of "Trying" by Joanna McCelland Glass. Tech Crew members were Isabel Cockle, Grace Dow, Baily Monteith, Fraser Nagle & Alex McKay who spent many hours prior to the February 2014 production working & learning with members of Thistle Theatre before opening night. The Valedictory Address was written & delivered by Fraser Nagle & Isabel Cockle. Warren McKay from McKay's Embro Food Market presented the plaques to these 2 talented youth who were chosen by their peers. Closing remarks were given by Julia Bujouves, principal. A social & dance were held following the awards. Farewells were at 10pm because there was school the next day.

Zorra Highland Park Graduation 2015

By Laura Green

Traditional Bagpipe music filled the Embro Community Centre as the Piper, Fraser Nagle piped the procession of graduates, staff & presenters into the hall filled with proud family members & flashing cameras. Principal Julia Bujouves, welcomed graduates & guests to this special evening on June 24, 2015. Anita Fraser representing Zorra Highland Park Parent Council/Home & School Association also gave remarks. Grade 8 teachers Rob Thrasher & Greg Willows presented the Recognition Certificates to the following students: Dylan Belore, Brady Bos, Reid Campbell, Ashleigh De Boer, Jenny Fletcher, Brittanie Fraser, Liam Fraser, Evan McIntosh, Robert McNiven, Calvin Munro, Rachel Murray, Abram Saunders, Jenna Tomen, Aimee Vey, Hailey Walker, Ella Westlake and Natalee Wilhelm. Honours Certificates were also presented by the Grade 8 teachers.

Academic Awards:

Drama ....Jenna Tomen
Sponsored by Thistle Theatre

Jacqueline Witteveen Memorial Art ....Rachel Murray
Sponsored by Witteveen Family

Music ....Ella Westlake

French ....Ella Westlake
Sponsored by Margaret Lupton

English ....Ella Westlake
Sponsored by Brooksdale Women's Institute

Mathematics ....Ashleigh De Boer
Sponsored by Don & Sharon Smith

Social Studies ....Rachel Murray
Sponsored by Anne & Al Matheson

Health & Physical Education...................Calvin Munro
Sponsored by Elgie Bus Lines Ltd

Male Athlete of the Year ....Dylan Belore
Sponsored by Elgie Bus Lines Ltd

Female Athlete of the Year ....Ella Westlake
Sponsored by Elgie Bus Lines Ltd

Science & Technology ....Ella Westlake
Sponsored by Harrington and Area Community Assoc.

Highest Academic......................................Ella Westlake
Sponsored by Ann & Dave Parker

Citizenship..Liam Fraser
Sponsored by Thistle Lodge No. 250

Perseverance ....Natalee Wilhelm
Sponsored by Zorra Caledonian Society

Jean Hossack Memorial Award.....................Liam Fraser
Sponsored by Ken Minler

Katelynn Innes Memorial Award ....Brittanie Fraser
Sponsored by Margo & Rick Innes

Arjen Pelders Memorial Award.............Robert McNiven
Sponsored by Oxford Farm Safety

Cody Henshaw Memorial Award.................Liam Fraser
Sponsored by Greenholm Farms

Principal's Award ....Ella Westlake

Dr. Gordon Murray Scholarships ....Ella Westlake
...........................Ashleigh De Boer and Brittanie Fraser

Chosen by their peers, Liam Fraser & Ashleigh De Boer were this year's Valedictorians. Plaques were presented by Warren McKay from McKay's Embro Food Market. In school activities, Ashleigh was a team member for the volleyball & basketball teams and she was involved in the year book committee. In the community Ashleigh plays on the Embro Soccer Team and with the Zorra Fusion Girl's Hockey team. In the fall she will be attending Woodstock Collegiate Institute. Liam Fraser is also a busy lad at school. He is a member of the tech crew, the orchestra & the volleyball team. He also runs the milk program. For after school activities, Liam is involved in the Air Cadets in Stratford and is taking bag pipe lessons with the Ingersoll Pipe band. He also volunteers at the Embro Tractor Pull and the Woodstock Flying Club Annual Garage Sale. In the fall Liam will be attend College Avenue Secondary School, Woodstock. Closing remarks were given by Principal Julia Bujouves ended the formal section. A social and dance followed until 10pm.

Embro Fire Station

After 33 years of service with Zorra Fire Rescue, Embro station, District Chief Bob Ross has decided to hang his fire helmet up, retiring to enjoy some quality time with his family and partake in the things he loves to do best. On behalf of the community and Zorra Fire Rescue we wish you all the best in your future endeavours.

Zorra Fire Rescue is proud to announce the promotion of Matt Cockle to District Chief of our Embro Station. His years as Deputy District Chief will serve him well in his new position. Assisting the District Chief in leadership duties, Captain Chris Schurman has been promoted to the position of Deputy District Chief. Matt, Chris and the Embro Fire Fighters are committed to the delivery of emergency services today and into the future.

Community Service Award 2014

By Laura Green

Richard and Robynn Donker are recipients of the 2014 Community Service Award. The Embro and Zorra Agricultural Society is always full of surprises and this year's annual meeting held January 20 at the Embro Legion was no exception. Robynn Donker was asked to make sure that her husband Richard would be attending the supper and AGM for he was going to receive the Community Service Award. Wow! Was she surprised to hear her name included in the announcement by presenter Al Kramer.

Their love story began at Ridgetown Agriculture College. According to Richard's two older brothers Robynn was a great influence on Richard. His marks improved tremendously and he was home on time for weekend chores on the family's dairy farm in the Embro area of Zorra Township.

After they were married and Richard developed his own herd of Holstein cattle, they built a new barn on their current farm not too far from the home farm. Robynn who was from Paris, Ontario, "married" into the Embro community and wanted to meet people and be involved in the community that her husband grew up in. In 2008,

she became a director for the Embro & Zorra Agricultural Society and is the current 1st Vice President of the main board. Robynn is involved with her church and with activities at their children's school, Zorra Highland Park. Richard soon discovered that "one meets more people at the fair, than cutting hay" when he helped Robynn with jobs at the fair like setting up all the display tables or putting up the miles of snow fence. He is currently an associate director for the fair board. Richard is the current President of Embro Minor Hockey and in previous years helped with the coaching. They want to demonstrate to their family of four young boys the importance of community involvement and how rewarding it can be.

Embro Dinner Theatre

Community Service Award 2015

By Laura Green

Embro & Zorra Agricultural Society held their annual meeting January 19, 2015. It was a complete surprise to Julie McIntosh when Past President Natalie Hazeleger announced her name as the 2015 Community Service Award recipient. Julie almost didn't come to the AGM, for her Uncle Robert was celebrating his 65th birthday on the same night. Julie began her involvement with the Embro Fair at a very young age, seven months in fact, for she was a participant in the Embro Fair's Baby Show. As the years passed, she entered items in the children's work and school work classes. Now you can find her jams and other canning items in the adult sections.

Her favourite area of the fair would be at the cattle sheds, helping her family prepare the dairy cattle for competition. She inherited her showmanship ability from both sides of her family tree. Julie started showing dairy calves in the Mayor of Zorra class, then joined the Bennington/Cody's 4-H Dairy Calf club when she turned 12-years-old. Now, she is a 4-H Volunteer (Leader) with the Dairy club and passes on her skills in showmanship to the next generation. She competed in many confirmation and showmanship classes, even at the Royal Winter Fair during her years as a 4-H youth member. Going off to the University of Guelph to earn her Bachelor of Science degree in Agriculture didn't stop her

involvement with fair. At the Embro Fair weekend, taking a break from her studies, one could find Julie in the cattle ring. Julie has been on the fair board for 12 years and during that time was President for two years and chaired many committees. She took 2014 off because of the constitution and now is officially installed as a director with lots of new ideas for 2015. Even in her "off" year, she chaired two committees and attended fair board meetings, she just couldn't vote. She has been involved with the Embro Dinner Theatre in many roles. She has produced productions, assistant stage managed, helped with set construction/design, bartended and served meals. For last two years, she was the kitchen convenor and played a crucial role in the transition from home craft division preparing the meal to finding a caterer. In the community, she has been involved with Thistle Theatre, on stage in some of their musicals and she produced their 2014 production "Having Hope at Home." Julie is very involved with the Knox United Church in Embro. She has been an elder, and sings in the church choir. Julie also sits on a board with the township looking to help our community/township/surrounding area attract new businesses and help existing businesses to flourish. When not travelling all over Canada with her full time job, she finds time for her family, friends and the family farm checking the pedigrees of the newest calves.

THAMESFORD

Harland B. Betzner Funeral Home

The following was printed in The Village Voice, May 2014

Thank You One And All

I would like to take this opportunity to announce my retirement from the Harland B. Betzner Funeral Home, effective April 1, 2014. I would also like to express my sincere thanks, gratitude and appreciation to the residents of Thamesford, Thorndale, Embro and Dorchester and surrounding areas for all the kindness, friendship, support and patronage over the past 41 plus years. My journey in Thamesford began on November 1, 1972, and being accepted and given the privilege to have served families in these communities over those years has been one of my greatest rewards. My decision to retire has not been taken lightly or without a great deal of consideration and thought. However, having worked for most part, on a 24/7 on call basis for all those years and having reached the age of 70 in January of this year, I have made the decision to "pass the torch" to the Brock and Visser Funeral Home of Woodstock in order to pursue and enjoy some personal time in my life. I cannot help but acknowledge so many groups and individuals that I have had the privilege and occasion to work with over the years as each circumstance necessitated; namely the clergy, cemeteries, medical staff, OPP, EMS as well as the Zorra Township Fire Service, which I had the privilege of being a part of for over 34 years. At this point, it is my intention to remain in Thamesford and be part of this community. So, in closing, may I once again express my thanks to each and every one of you for your thoughtfulness & friendship. It truly is appreciated.

Sincerely, Harland Betzner

Harland displaying his natural musical talent with his cohorts: Paul Golding, George Houlton, Sy Glover, (Harland with the mouth organ), Howard Sims and Arnold the pig (who stole the show at a performance in Lucan).

Mission Possible Trip to Haiti

Honouring September 2015 Visit to Haiti and Dominican Republic

By Bud and Donna Gillam

The journey began at 4am on September 3, flying from Detroit to Miami, then on to Port-au-Prince. The flights were great.

After we landed, we piled our luggage in the middle of the stake truck and found our spot on the benches on each side and clung on for the long bumpy ride ahead. The vehicle we rode in was well secured with a covered roof and mesh sides that were open to the elements. Wind, rain and dust, we experienced them all. Due to demonstrations in the City of Arcahaie, the direct road was closed. So our route turned inland. The five hour ride took us through the mountains, over a recent mud slide and north to St Marc. We then headed south down the coast to Montrouis and then it was welcome to Haiti! When we arrived at the Mission Possible Compound at about 10pm, a delicious meal was waiting for us, which we quickly devoured. We were then gently lulled to sleep by the waves. It was a very long day of travel.

One purpose for our trip was to celebrate the graduation of our first Leadership Academy students. These folks currently hold leadership positions with Mission Possible - our school nurse, school directors, principals and pastors. The intensive 20 month course of training covered various aspects to improve and equip these leaders - striving to bring excellence in our schools and churches. Students in cap and grown were individually honoured as they received their diplomas in traditional pomp and ceremony, then challenged to share the knowledge they had received, continue learning and developing their own personal growth. Families were invited to celebrate the achievements of their loved ones and a warm reception followed. A job well done!

Haiti is a land of opportunity. Micro enterprise is everywhere, kids will sell you a bag of ice, water or fruit drinks for just a few gourdes. One gourd equals about 3¢ Canadian. You can see almost anything in a wheel barrel or on the back of a motorbike, including four other passengers, pigs, goats, furniture, building supplies and on and on. Somethings never change like Tap-taps jammed with people going somewhere, trucks piled high over the side racks with cargo then people sitting on top and they are always driving too fast.

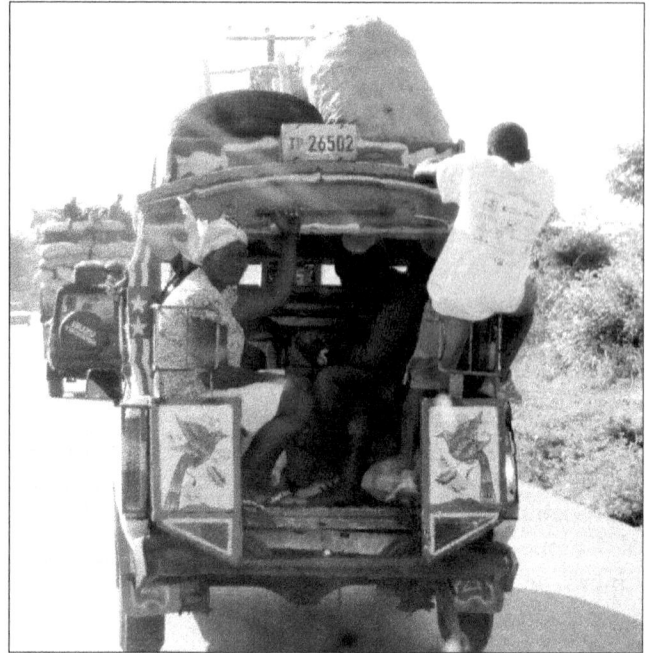

Outside of Port-au-Prince many of the new townhouse or apartment buildings we saw were laying unfinished for some reason. Did the organization building them run out of funds or is there another reason? There are pockets of progress which is encouraging but much is still to be done. Crossing the border into the D.R. is an adventure in itself. Our Ebenezer School and Churches are located in Barahona and our team was invited to attend the first evening church service in their partially finished building, complete with lights and power. It was a joyous occasion for all! The next day at the school we took photos of all the kids, always an enjoyable job. Visit www.OurMissionIsPossible for more info about Child Sponsorship and the ministry to schools and churches in Haiti and the Dominican Republic or call us at 519-285-2644. Mission Possible is - "Equipping the next generation of Christ-centered Leaders".

Detroit Mission Work

By Larry Edwards, Minister, Parish of the Thames, St. John's Thamesford, St. George's Thorndale, St. Luke's Crumlin, Christ Church Lakeside.

"Detroit was once one of the greatest cities in the world. The birthplace of the American auto industry, by the 1950's it boasted the highest median income & the highest rate of home ownership of any major American city." (from USA Today). As the auto manufacturers went into decline, life in Detroit changed forever. People were laid off, never to be recalled to well paying jobs. The long term consequences for working class people were heartbreaking. People with the skills and ability to move to other cities left in droves. Property values plummeted as hundreds of thousands of homes went up for sale. Those left behind, too old or unwilling to move for whatever reason, were left to fend for themselves. They say that one house in four has been abandoned in Detroit. On some blocks, there may be two or three houses in disrepair. On others, every other house will be beyond saving. In the homes remaining, live desperate people, mainly African Americans. Where we stay and work, the majority of the people seem to be elderly pensioners. There are some young people, often wives and children of families without fathers and husbands. With the loss of most of their tax base the city of Detroit is now unable to supply many of the basic services one would expect. Streets not repaired. Parks are overgrown with grass and weeds. The response time for emergency services is very slow. There is no money for all the thousands who would be on social assistance here in Ontario. In response to this need, Rev. Carl Zerweck began an outreach mission to Detroit five years ago. Carl has been doing outreach work all over America for the past 20 years. He and his wife organize and oversee mission trips. Carl had planned on this being a one year event, he would do as much as he could in one summer and then move on. But when he realized how desperate the people of Detroit were he decided to move to Detroit and make this an ongoing mission. The organization is called Rippling Hope Ministries and you can learn all about it on the internet. St. John's Anglican Church, Thamesford has been sending volunteers to Detroit for five years now. Groups who come to Rippling Hope are provided with all the tools, materials and training to do various jobs. Jobs range from painting, fence building, yard cleanups, boarding up houses, cleaning eaves troughs, caulking windows and more. The home owners must pay for most of the materials and the labour is done by volunteers. This is an excellent mission opportunity for people who want to help build the kingdom of God here on earth while bringing hope to people who think they are alone and forgotten. It is amazing to me that there are thousands of desperate people just a two hour drive from this area and yet

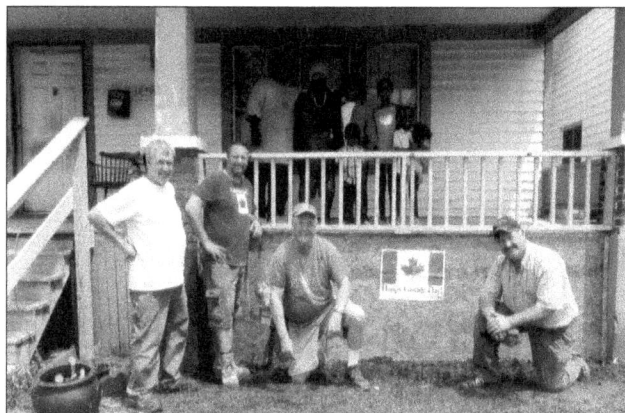

Left to right work crew, Dave Salhani and Kevin Rye Thamesford, Larry Edwards Aymer, Ken Otto, North Zorra. Above, Mrs. Brown her by her daughter and grandchildren.

people are spending thousands of dollars to travel to far flung destinations to do mission work. Jesus said "love your neighbour" maybe he meant it literally. The people of Detroit are our neighbours, our close neighbours! Let me close with a few examples of the people we met and the work we did. At one home an elderly widow couldn't use her back door steps to go out and hang her wash on the line. The steps were rotted and not safe. For years she has been carrying her laundry basket out the front door, around the side of the house, and out into the back yard to dry them. We replaced the steps and added a railing. She was so thankful. Another elderly couple had a broken lock on their front door. They would pile furniture up against the door and then sleep in fear of being robbed. We replaced that lock in just a few minutes. At another home we met Mrs. Brown, an elderly widow living on a fixed income of $250 a month. She has her daughter and grandchildren living with her. Mrs. Brown loves to sit out on her porch but it was in terrible condition, not safe for anyone to walk on. Our group replaced all the floor boards, put new supports under the porch, added a railing and boarded up the crawl space. Mrs. Brown had saved up $400 to buy the materials but a recent flooded basement had required her to spend her porch money. When we learned of her misfortune our congregations provided the money to complete the repairs on her porch. We finished the work on Mrs. Brown's porch on Canada Day. We were proud to pin the Canada Day Flag to the porch as Mrs. Brown's family and our work crew posed for a photograph of the completed job. Volunteering in Detroit with Rippling Hope is a very rewarding experience, I would recommend it to any church or service organization. To give you an idea how affordable these trips are, a 3 day work trip, tools and jobs provided and organized, four nights accommodation complete with all meals costs only $150 U.S. A full week is just $350 U.S.

Just For You Bed & Breakfast Celebrates

BED & BREAKFAST

The 10 year anniversary of Just 4 You Bed and Breakfast located outside of Thamesford was celebrated in 2014. "It's an interesting business," said owner, Ron Bouwman. "You meet a lot of people." Some people come in all frazzled from dealing with the day to day stresses of life. "We like to pamper them and then they start to relax and enjoy themselves."

Ron said that it is not all that different to the health care industry. Something he and partner Gerrard Hamoen were both familiar with. Ron and Gerard, who have been together for more than 30 years, both worked as nurses in Holland before they immigrated to Canada. They first took up residence in Tillsonburg in October 2003.

In Holland they had an beautiful house located on a full acre with amazing gardens. It was located in the middle of the Centre Park of Holland with picturesque nature trails around it. They also had a garden house that was heated with running water and all amenities but Ron said they never considered renting it out as a bed and breakfast. "Every one declared us crazy when we said we were moving to Canada," said Ron. "Holland's a beautiful book but I had read it."

Ron was ready for a move. He said it took Gerard a little longer to come around to the idea but they both decided to make the move. At the time of their application, nurses were not needed so Ron and Gerard couldn't apply as professionals. They decided to develop a business plan and apply as self employed. They originally were looking at opening a boarding kennel for dogs and cats as well as a bed and breakfast.

Once they had moved, they looked at their plan again and decided that the kennel was going take too long to establish and that they would focus solely on the bed and breakfast. Hospitality had been a field that Gerard had a lot of interest in. "So we decided to forget about the kennel and put all the eggs into the basket of the bed and breakfast," said Ron. All the money they had saved for the kennel was now going to be used towards the bed and breakfast.

Ron and Gerard found the property outside of Thamesford and took possession of it in December 2003. Although a new house, a lot of work had to be done to make it into the place Ron and Gerard envisioned. They worked really hard painting and decorating and getting the house ready for guests.

In April of 2004 they opened with two rooms, but then decided to gut and rebuild. "There was lots of upgrading and turning it around to suit our purposes," said Ron. Now their bed and breakfast offers four rooms, each with their own private bathrooms and separate entrances. Two are regular rooms while the other two are suites that feature kitchenettes. "We had visited a lot of bed and breakfasts over the years. We took all those good experiences and tried to incorporate them into our place."

Ron and Gerard have included a lot of amenities for their guests to enjoy. "Really we have everything a big hotel does but here you are not just a number." They believe it is the extra pampering touches that provide their guests with that much needed break. They have a sauna, hot tub, pool, exercise equipment, table hockey, fireplace and surround sound big screen TV area. Added touches of fresh fruit and flowers as well as chocolates probably contribute to the fact they have so many returning guests.

Ron will have more time to spend helping Gerard with the business now that he has retired from nursing at University Hospital in London. He started there shortly after they came to Canada which made the Thamesford location a great spot.

Apart from meeting the interesting people, one of Ron's other favourite things about the bed and breakfast is that the extra income helped him retire. "I have worked my whole life since I was 17 in health care. I was happy to retire last year at the age of 60."

In 2015, all their hard efforts paid off. Ron and Gerard won a Trip Advisor Certificate of Excellence award. It was awarded to them for their hospitality and for achieving great reviews on TripAdvisor. "There is no greater seal of approval than being recognized by one's customers."

St. Joseph's School, Thamesford Closes

By Tony Kelly

The founding meeting to build a Roman Catholic primary school to serve the children of area residents was held at the home of Jerry Moyer. Among those attending were Rev. Fr. Joseph Brisson, Parish Priest of Sacred Heart, Ingersoll, Leo Woodcroft, Sid Doran, Harry Vader, Peter Poel, Tony Kelly, John Poel, Tom Hann and a number of residents from the surrounding area. Fr. Brisson announced that it was time for Thamesford to have a separate school due to the increasing number of children who would be able to attend. The question of a location was answered when Fr. Brisson stated that the London Diocese had purchased 10 acres (6 for a church and 4 for a school).

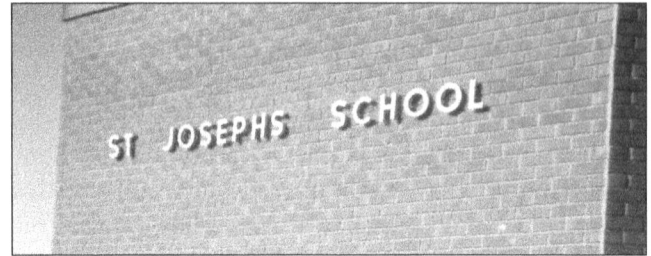

St. Joseph's School's grade 7 and 8 class, June 1990.

A school design suitable for Thamesford had been completed in Avon by Wallace Bros.

The name St. Joseph's came easily as both Fr. Joseph Brisson and Fr. Joseph Baggatto were involved.

Miss Eva O'Neill and Mrs. Mazzerole had expressed willingness to teach at St. Joe's. To increase the number of available students, satellite boards were established with students being bussed to Thamesford by Stuart Elgie.

The first graduate was Terry Doran in 1964 or 1965, Numbers attending increased with an extention. Two more rooms and a gym were added in the 1970's. The Oxford Roman Catholic Board converted the electric heating to boilers, town water and sewers were installed.

The school was an integral part of Thamesford as evidenced by the Thanksgiving turley dinners, village sports and Calithumpian parades. The school choirs were an important part of the Thamesford Lions Community Carol sings each year, right up until the school closing. The school also played a vital part in the ecology as seen in the trees, plants and the Peace Garden. Finally, the lack of new enrolment caused the closing of a force for education in Oxford.

The following was printed in The Village Voice, June 2014

ST JOSEPH'S SCHOOL OPEN HOUSE

Calling all community members past & present... St Joseph's Catholic Elementary School in Thamesford is closing. We want to celebrate its 50 years of existence, education and nurturing faith. Please join us for fellowship, remembrance and look back at the precious life of a little school community. Every is welcome. Formal gathering at 6pm in the gymnasium. Share your memories, reconnect. Refreshments provided.

The following was printed in The Village Voice, July 2014

IT TAKES A VILLAGE TO RAISE A CHILD
(African Proverb)
As the doors close at St Joseph's Catholic School, Thamesford and new & exciting opportunities unfold, we as staff & students would like to thank Thamesford & extended area for all of your support over the 50 years of Catholic education at our school.
From individuals, businesses & service clubs to parents, friends, family friends & others, we want to say "Thank You." We could not have done it without you!

Truth Community Church Opens

In the fall of 2013, a group of men, women and children met at a farm house, outside of Thamesford. They were a rather large group to fit in one house, around 50 people. They were of all different ages and backgrounds, but all had one thing in common: they desired to start a brand new church. There are certainly a lot of great churches all around already, but this group was close knit and really felt that God was leading them to start a new church and in time really came to the belief that Thamesford was the place for them to "set up shop".

At first they met in the garage of this farm house, having a Thanksgiving dinner after their first Sunday meeting together as a church on October 13, 2013. While this was exciting and fun, the lack of heat in the garage proved to make it hard for people to not freeze. During this time, Crossroads Alliance Church invited them to use their building on Sunday afternoons. Over the first number of months, the new church family met in a total of eight different locations. Eventually they were able to settle in at the former St. Joseph's Catholic School after the school closed in June of 2014.

After starting up and meeting for a while, the church decided to invite Rev. Shawn Robinson to come and be their pastor. Pastor Shawn and his family joined in with this new group and Shawn took on the role of pastor about three months after the church started. One of the early decisions was simply picking a name. What name did they want to be known as for years to come? The new church collected over 20 suggestions from the people, but as they evaluated the names they began to think of something that Jesus said. At one point, Jesus declared, "I am the way, the truth and the life. No one comes to the Father except through me" (John 14:6). They thought of the love and kindness of Jesus and realized that when you have the Truth of who Jesus is, what he is like, what he is really all about… you have love, kindness, grace, mercy - all the good stuff! They decided that naming the church "Truth Community Church" (TCC) would be a way to declare what they are really all about, "Jesus!"

As a church, TCC had been praying about purchasing St. Joseph's School. This was a big step of faith for the people of this new church, but the Lord provides! In the summer of 2015, TCC took possession of the building and moved right in!

The people in the church began showing up to paint and fix stuff. The youth group began to meet at the new building and take advantage of the gym, and the church family began to make use of more and more of the building! TCC has a great desire to not just meet as a church in Thamesford, but to be a part of the community. They have rented the ice rink and offered free public skating as a way to connect up and love the community as well as taken part in parades and other community events. Thamesford really is a wonderful community and it's a privilege to be a part of it!

As a church, Truth Community Church is all about loving people and loving Jesus. They are a group of imperfect people who are trying to look to Jesus in everything. Thank you all for the privilege of being a part of such a great village and a special thanks to those who have been so encouraging and helpful to us as we've navigated through starting a new church. People like our friends at Crossroads, Doug Mills and all his help with rentals, the Lions Club with the carol sing, the Calithumpian committee, the Catholic School Board, Marion at St. John's Anglican Church and more! And thanks to God for all his leading and love through the first 2 years of being a new church!

Truth
COMMUNITY CHURCH

www.truthcommunitychurch.ca

The Fisher's of Thamesford
Help Break A Guinness World Record

By Sharyn Fisher, Thamesford

On August 14, Bob and I left home at 4 a.m. to travel to St. Albert, near Casselman, Ontario. We were headed for an amazing adventure with our trailer loaded with our mini threshing machine. After over 600kms we arrived at our destination. Almost two inches of rain fell before our arrival and everything was muddy. A man from Embrun, Francois Latour, had a vision of breaking the current record in the Guinness Book of World Records record set in Saskatchewan of 45 threshing machines running at the same time. Saturday, August 15 was a hot and humid day. We also had the mud to contend with. The steam engine's whistle blew at exactly 12 noon and we began threshing of barley 15 minutes. Francois' dream had come true with 111 out of 115 machines all threshing at the same time! What a sight to see and what an amazing experience to have been part of with over 5,000 people in attendance. Francois' wife, only aged 49, had been battling breast cancer for over a year and all the money raised from this project is going to fight breast cancer. Francois broke the 2014 record, but later Saturday afternoon, his wife died. A dream and a nightmare for Francois all in the same day.

Garry Montgomery and Bob Fisher

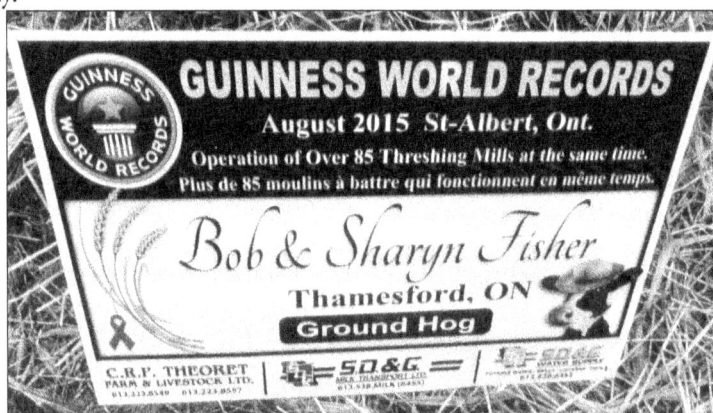

A row of antique wooden threshing machines

A crowd of over 5,000 spectators.

Doing it the old way...

Sharyn Fisher

The end product

59

Fund Raising for Muscular Dystrophy

*Thamesford residents Justice and Kaidince Sweeney, both of whom have Muscular Dystrophy,
are presented a cheque for $1,000 for Muscular Dystrophy Canada
by members of Zorra Fire & Emergency Services - Thamesford Station*

Our thanks go out to the Sweeney Family for their help at our car wash and to everyone
who supports the Fire Fighters in their annual fundraising efforts

45th Anniversary
of the 1st Great Ride for Cancer

Thamesford Legion Closes

The proceeds from the sale of the Thamesford Legion building were donated back to several non-profit organizations in and around the community on January 16, 2015 at the Thamesford Trojans hockey game. The membership at our last meeting made these recommendations and Dominion Command had the final say. The members at that meeting included Bob Fisher, Bruce Gordon, Garry Bennett, Tammy Hooper, Tyler McCready, Kale Patience, Eric Gledhill and Gary Pounds. Ted Scott our Zone Commander was in charge of the proceeding. Ontario Command said they would donate 66% of the remaining money to the community. Because most of the money came from this community we wanted it to go back to this community. Almost everyone has a child, grandchild, or great grandchild that will benefit from this money. Robb Kersel received a cheque for $1,000 on behalf of the Zorra Girl's Hockey Assoc. Tammy Spriel and Francine Overeem accepted a cheque for $7,000 on behalf of Thamesford Minor hockey. Lisa Teeple accepted a cheque for $8,000 on behalf of Thamesford Minor Baseball. Wade Schaefer accepted a cheque for $8,000 on behalf of Thamesford Minor Soccer. A cheque will be donated to Jackie Vandaele who could not attend for $8,000 on behalf of the 1st Thamesford/Kintore Scouting. Heather Muir accepted a cheque for $8,000 on behalf of the Girl Guides of Canada 2nd Thamesford Brownies and Guides. Brenda Cole accepted a cheque for $8,000 for the Thamesford Skating Club. Steve Glover accepted a cheque for $8,000 on behalf of the Thamesford Trojans. Andrea Wright accepted a cheque for $15,000 on behalf of the Thamesford Calithumpian Weekend. A cheque for $5,000 will be presented to Tammy Hooper on behalf of the 201 Dorchester Air Cadets by Ted Scott at their next meeting. We trust that all the organizations will make good use of this much needed money. Thank you to everyone who supported the Thamesford Legion over the years.

A GOOD THAMESFORD STORY...

Appeared in the September 2014 Thamesford Village Voice

Two Thamesford girls were going up in a gondola car to the top of a mountain in Ecuador. There was a man sitting beside them who came from Germany, he asked where the girls came from "We are from Canada" the girls answered. Oh, said the man, "I was there once, I worked in Thamesford for Harvey Beaty." The girls just looked at each other - what was there to say except - "Well, that's were we live!!!"

Westminster United Church Theatre

2014

WESTMINSTER
UNITED CHURCH THAMESFORD

PROUDLY PRESENTS

Nunsense II
The second coming...

Book, Music & Lyrics by
Dan Goggin

Performed by Arrangement with Tams-Witmark Music, New York, NY

Dinner Theatre 6:00 pm
Balcony Seating 7:00 pm
November 6, 7, 8 & 9, 2014

November 8th **Matinee 1:00 pm**
November 9th **Lunch Theatre 12 Noon**

2015

WESTMINSTER
UNITED CHURCH THAMESFORD

PROUDLY
PRESENTS

By L. Frank Baum
With Music and Lyrics
by Harold Arlen and E. Y. Harburg
Background Music by Herbert Stothart
Dance and Vocal Arrangements by Peter Howard
Orchestration by Larry Wilcox
Adapted by John Kane for the Royal Shakespeare Company
Based upon the Classic Motion Picture
owned by Turner Entertainment Co.
and distributed in all media by Warner Bros.

Dinner Theatre 6:00 pm
Balcony Seating 7:30 pm
November 5-14, 2015
November 8th   Matinee 2:00 pm
November 10 & 12 - Traditional Theatre 7:00 pm

62

Habitat Home for Thamesford Family

The following was printed in The Village Voice

A hand up, not a hand out

Habitat for Humanity Heartland is starting a build in the fall of 2015 in Ingersoll. The groundwork for this project is well underway. A local family of five has been selected and is looking forward to moving into their new home.

In addition, a lot has been purchased on Bell St. and generous support has been received from the community and local contractors. Please consider giving a "hand up" to this deserving family and together, let's turn their dream of owning a home of their own into a reality. The website is habitat4home.ca/build/Oxford/Ingersoll/Margaret St. Habitat for Humanity Heartland Ontario is a non-prof-

it, non-denominational Christian housing organization. We welcome partners without discrimination to help us build simple, decent, affordable homes with low-income families. 100% of the ReStores revenue supports the administrative costs of Habitat for Humanity Heartland Ontario. We believe that by offering a family a hand-up, not a hand-out, we empower low-income families to become successful homeowners. Habitat Heartland Ontario is an affiliate of Habitat for Humanity Canada, who works with corporate, individual and faith-based donors and volunteers to help low-income families realize a more stable future through the home ownership program.

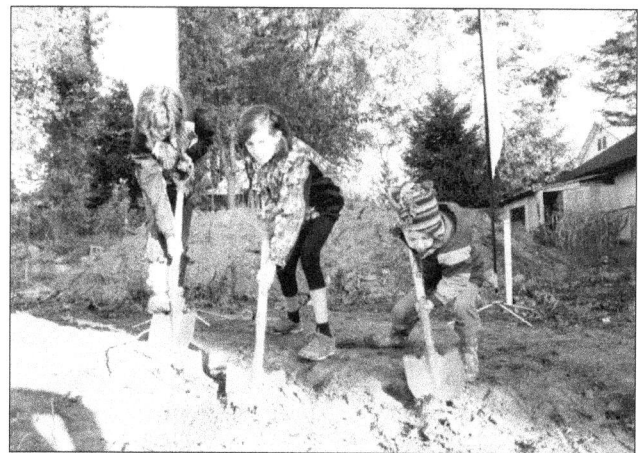

The official groundbreaking event for Ingersoll's next Habitat for Humanity build took place October 8, 2015. A new home for Craig & Krista Sweeney and their family will be ready in the spring of 2016.

Norm Lansdell - A Century of Memories

The following was printed in The Village Voice

Happy 100th birthday to Norm Lansdell January 6, 2016! Norm was born in London township and was the second oldest of 3 brothers. His parents immigrated to Canada in 1903 from Norfolk, England. He has resided within the Thamesford area since 1963. He was married to Mary (Dec 5, 2015) for 63 years. Together, they had 4 children, 13 grandchildren and 3 great grandchildren. Norm worked as a blacksmith with his father, served as a lieutenant in the Canadian army during WW II and owned a construction business before buying the family farm. Norm has always been an active Anglican church member at St. Luke's, Crumlin and St. John's, Thamesford. Not only has he served as warden, synod rep and reader, but he continues to play the mandolin at special services. He has also done countless carpentry/renovation work over the years as well as co-found / cook at the annual chicken BBQs. His health is remarkably good, which could be attributed to being physically/mentally active, helping others & having good genes. Norm's mother (1983) lived to be 107 years old. He continues to be involved with 5 masonic lodges, including the Mocha Shrine and has enjoyed his band-playing years with The Glengarys, a local musical group. He is also Past President of the Oxford Soil/Crop and Oxford Co Cattleman's Associations. 1976 was the year that he was crowned Oxford County Corn Silage King. Public celebrations of Norm's 100th birthday were held at St. John's Church and the Mocha Shrine Centre. Printed acknowledgements were received from the Queen, Governor General, Prime Minister, Premier, MP & MPP (Oxford County), Mayor (Zorra Township), Veteran's Affairs and the Grand Lodge of Canada. Norm offers simple advice to younger generations: "Be kind, help each other and show gratitude." Congratulations and thank you, Norm, for all that you have done for your family, neighbours, community and country. A wonderful milestone!

ge 10, Town Crier, August 31,1978

DISCUSSING AGRICULTURE ISSUES — Members of the Oxford soils and crop improvement association kept Eugene Whelan, the federal minister of agriculture, under a steady barrage of questions at the farm of Normasn Lansdell. Whelan told the members he would try and rescue the Can Farm program, recently cut, from extinction.

IT. NOM 2MO

Vol 1 No. 40   AUG. 31 1978.   THAMESFORD

MINISTER PRESENTS FLAG — Eugene Whelan, federal minister of agriculture, presented Edith Lansdell with a Canadian flag in honor of her recent 102 birthday on Monday.

Here's what was happening the year Norm was born...

- Canada's original Parliament buildings in Ottawa burned down

- Women were allowed to attend a boxing match

- Easter Rising of Irish republicans against British occupation begins in Dublin

- Daylight Savings time is introduced

- Indianapolis 500: Dario Resta wins in 3:34:16.990 (135.187 km/h)

- Mary Pickford becomes the first female film star to get a million dollar contract

- John D. Rockefeller becomes the first billionaire

- Margaret Sanger opens 1st birth control clinic (46 Amboy St, Brooklyn). She is later arrested for obscenity (advocating birth control).

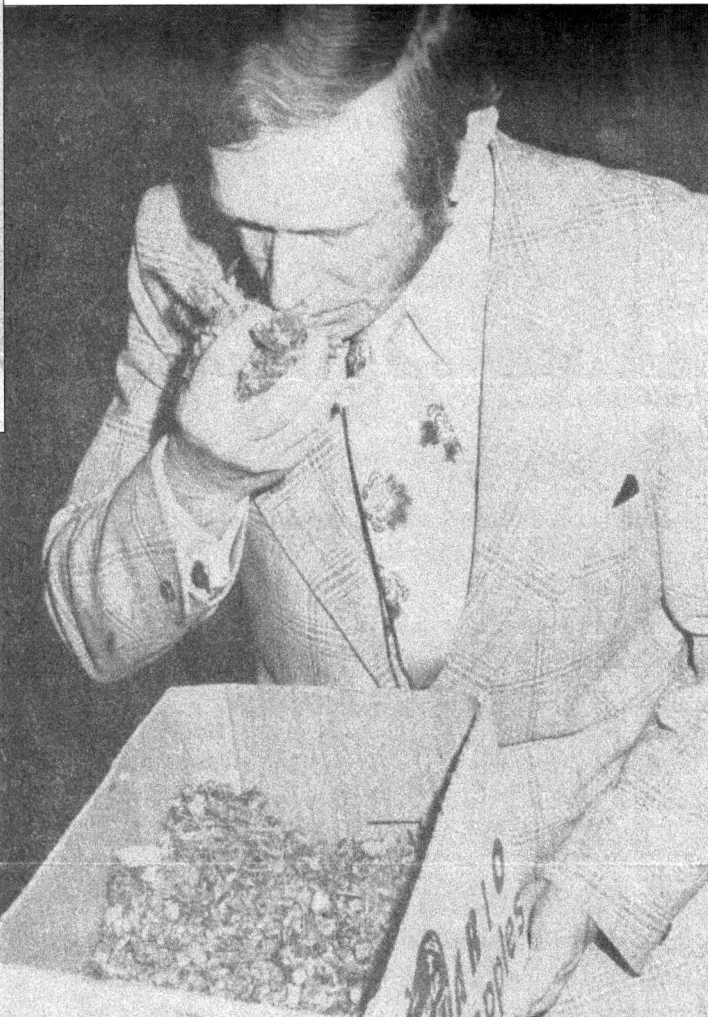

Corn King tests flavor of winning corn by smelling it.
(Staff photo by Tim McKenna)

Silage King picked

By JANICE VANSICKLE
Sentinel-Review Staff Writer

Oxford County's new Corn Silage King is Norman Lansdell.

Lansdell, a Thamesford area farmer took top prize in the whole plant silage class.

He attributed his win to luck.

He said he didn't do anything special to win.

"I just put my corn in the silo and happeneed to come across some really good silage at the time of the show," he said.

He did say, however, that he collected 442 points of a possible 500. His nearest competitor had 431 points.

Lansdell also won first prize in the shelled corn class, but finished near the bottom in one of the hay classes, the only other class he entered.

The "king" didn't try to take advantage of his reign.

Shortly after learning of his win, he had a broom in his hands to sweep up scraps of hay that had tumbled on the floor of the Oxford Auditorium during the judging of the hay classes at

good hay," Knabe said, adding: "No matter what kind of contest you're in, you've got to go for first."

COMPETING

He has been competing in the feed fair for about 15 years and last year he won third prize in the second hay cutting class, the class he won this year.

Knabe also tied with three other farmers as runner-up to the silage king, collecting 430 of a possible 500 points.

Clare Hartley, Woodstock, and Bill MacIntosh, Embro, each collected 430 points, as

65

Farewell to Thamesford Mill

For more than a century the Thamesford Mill, perched by the damn at the Thames River. It was a focal point of the village of Thamesford. The mill was the landmark you saw as you drove down Dundas Street through Thamesford. It was a part of the community with a history that spanned more than 150 years.

The original wooden mill was built in 1845 but was destroyed by fire in 1898. The brick structure which stood until 2014 was built in 1898.

The mill site had been the location for Finkle's Mill, which first served as a grist mill and later a sawmill before becoming known as Cawthorpe's Mill and then eventually as Hogg's Mill.

It was one of the first major economic forces in the former Township of East Nissouri. The mill not only provided flour but also income for farmers selling grain and timber there. It also acted as a place of employment for many local residents.

At one time the mill's four floors of well-maintained machinery produced four hundred 98lb bags of flour per day and relied entirely on water power. Later on electrical power was used to assist operation during low water flow periods.

In 1970 the mill relied completely on electrical power. 1971 was the year that the mill was sold to Maple Leaf Feeds and operated as a feed mill and warehouse. In 1990 the mill closed. In 2007 the property changed hands again. A tough decision was made by its owners and the structure was demolished in 2014.

Although many will miss this landmark building that has stood guard over the Thames River for generations, its history is represented at the Beachville District Museum and a lengthy and well-documented story of the Thamesford Mill can be found in the East Nissouri History Book located at the Thamesford Library.

TIMELINE

1845	Thamesford Mill is built.
1898	Fire destroys original wooden structure, current buildings are constructed.
1990s	Operations cease at the site.
2012	Demolition begins.
2014	An approved zoning change turns the site into highway commercial property instead of industrial.
2015	Dewy's Auto moves from further down Dundas Street and opens May 1, 2015 in the newly revamped warehouse portion of the former mill buildings.

Thamesford Fire Station

Sod turning ceremony at the site of the new fire hall in Thamesford

*From left: Thamesford Fire Chief John McFarlan, Councillor Marcus Ryan, Mayor Margaret Lupton,
Councillor Marie Keasey, Councillor Ron Forbes*

*December 2015
The new fire hall nears completion.*

67

Calithumpian 2015

THAMESFORD LONG WEEKEND CELEBRATIONS ~ JOIN US!

MAY 17TH

DEMOLITION DERBY!

Derby contact Andrea Wright 519-285-5129

MAY FRI. 16TH - MON. 19TH

HOME RUN DERBY

FRIDAY MAY 15TH 6-9PM
THAMESFORD NORTH PARK
ALL AGE CATEGORIES CONTACT
BETHANY BARR 519-868-3583

KEEP CALM AND CALI ON

FIREWORKS

SUN. MAY 17TH Rain date Mon. May 18

AT DUSK THAMESFORD REC CENTRE

ROAD HOCKEY TOURNEY

SATURDAY MAY 16TH
PRE-REGISTRATION REQ'D
CONTACT TAMMY BETZNER 519-670-1280

PRINCESS & SUPERHERO PARTY SAT. MAY 16TH 2-4PM

THAMESFORD REC HALL CONTACT ANDREA WRIGHT 519-285-5129

PARADE MON. MAY 18TH 1PM

Route on back of flyer.

BEST FAMILY FLOAT

Get Your Families Together to Make a Great Float!

$250 CASH PRIZE FOR BEST FAMILY FLOAT

Contact Jen Beattie 519-285-2846 for Parade

Sponsored by **Brock & Visser**, Thamesford Funeral Home

TEENAGERS NEED HOURS? WE NEED YOU!

Dr. Kosmal Dedication Ceremony

The public was welcomed to gather Sunday, August 17, 2014, as they dedicated the park area in honour Dr. Richard Kosmal and his dedication to the village of Thamesford. The TBA, the Thamesford Lions Club and the Township of Zorra all contributed to this beautiful park to commemorate Dr. Richard and Marion Kosmal's memory. The Kosmal Family lovingly contributed the 2 yellow benches & the unique plaques to honour their parents. We welcomed the Kosmal family and the people of Thamesford to join us as we opened this beautiful passive area.

KOSMAL PARK OPENING

Pauline, Nick & Jazzmine Kosmal listen as Wendy Lake shared with those who gathered for the dedication of Dr. Kosmal Park on August 17, 2014.

Dr. Kosmal practiced medicine in the Thamesford area for many years.

He had a family practitioner's office located on the main street in Thamesford.

THAMESFORD

TBA

BUSINESS ASSOCIATION

The Thamesford Business Association

"A group dedicated to making Thamesford an attractive and prosperous place to do business."

OUR PROJECTS:

- Christmas Raffle Basket
- Farm Fresh Market
- Yellow Benches & Planters
- Flower Gardens on the Main Street
- Thamesford.org website
- Thamesford Banners
- 'Lily' Award for garden efforts by citizens
- Thamesford Entrance Signs
- Village Christmas Decorations
- Festival of Lights for decorating efforts by citizens
- Thamesford Facebook page
- Annual Golf Tournament

In the beginning, the Thamesford Business Association was not really a business association, but, rather a "sort of" men's club made up of business men. This was started by G.D. Jefferson (lawyer) who asked Ron Hogg, Dr. Kosmal, Audie Ruby, Sy Glover and George Nelson to be founding members. Bern Cummings was also asked as she was the constant at the bank seeing the managers were always being transferred. Eventually this group became the Thamesford Business Association.

Harland Betzner was an early member of this group and in his own words:

"The mission of the TBA was to promote respect and harmony throughout all the businesses of Thamesford."

Do you remember these businesses in Thamesford?

- Oliver's Hardware Store
- The Golden Touch
- Dippy's Ice Cream
- The Cheese House
- 1001 Bargains
- Lorna's Closet Boutique & Tea Room
- Sears Order Office & Antique Store
- Flowers by Leanne
- Smith's Furniture
- The Balmoral Hotel
- John Wright Motors
- Bill Dempsey's Variety
- Wally Kortz Appliances
- Fina Gas Station
- Dunc Hossack's Chrysler Dealership
- Hogg's Feed Mill
- McLeods Grocery Store
- Purple Hill Meats
- Shewan Meats
- Master Feeds
- Weir's Sport Store
- the original JC Graphics
- Ron Hogg Real Estate
- London Business Machines
- Dr. R. Kosmal
- G.D. Jefferson
- Texaco Gas Station
- The Town Lunch
- Shewan's Barber Shop
- Gilbert Fuels
- The Butcher Block
- Carruthers Funeral Home

2015 banner design.

Thamesford banners hang on the main streets of the town. The banners are purchased by businesses and individuals and feature a name at the bottom of the banner.

This has proven a successful way for community members to support the TBA in their efforts to beautify the town. Above is the newly designed for banners that hang in the village in 2015.

TBA 5th Annual Lily Award – 2014

The Thamesford Business Associations Garden Lily Award acknowledges
residents whose gardens enhance our village.

Our choices for 2014 (in no particular order) are:

KATHY WAYNE & MIKE PATTERSON
198 Delatre Street

Kathy and Mike spend many hours weekly in maintaining their beautiful backyard. They have over 250 plants and when in full-bloom they are gorgeous. Complete with a garden encircling a tree shared by their neighbours they have planted hostas & flowers which are complimentary to both sides – they call this area their "Circle of Friends". Blue adirondack chairs sitting on a small flagstone patio invites you to relax with a cup of tea, a glass of wine and a good book or just to sit and gaze over their private oasis.

DARLENE & BILL ATKINSON
68 Sloan Drive

Bill & Darlene have lived in the new subdivision for 14 years and have designed & built every detail of their yard. From entering through a wrought iron gate, along a flagstone walkway which draws you toward a rockery waterfall, a trellis filled with beautiful pink & purple clematis, contoured and manicured beds filled with a variety of flowers & a 2nd water feature to lull you into relaxing in their outdoor living room / gazebo.

SHIRLEY & JOHN CLEMENTE
157 Stanley Street N.

Beautiful lawns, manicured & contoured gardens with a variety of trees and plants, 2 complimentary planters with a blooming array of yellow begonias set off the facade & highlight the front entranceway to this home. The colours continue along the side of the house and into the back yard along an interlocking stone walkway. This home creates such an enchanting invitation to knock on their front door.

TBA 6th Annual Lily Award – 2015

The Thamesford Business Association, once again, had a very exciting tour around our village to choose 3 homes that exuded drive-by appeal with manicured gardens, ornamentation, colour & a welcoming invitation to "knock on their door". This year we had 10 homes on our list & we had the difficult job of narrowing this down to 3.
Our choices for 2015 (in no particular order) are:

KELLY & COSIMO CIRIELLO
37 Oliver Cres.
A lovely home in the new subdivision with beautiful purple clematis climbing up the wall, huge lava rocks in the front flower beds, surrounded by manicured shrubs, sedum, stella dora & lilies. Two lions on the veranda are guarding the front door, but, they wouldn't stop you from dropping in for a visit. Kelly was the first to admit that Cosimo was the gardener and deserved all the credit.

DOROTHY FORBES
135 Allen St.
This beautiful home is overlooking the river with well-cared for & lush manicured lawns. The variegated hostas, hydrangeas & pops of colour with huge red geraniums & yellow begonias make it a bright gateway into our village. When delivering the lily, Dorothy explained that all the geraniums were from last year, which she hung in her cold room throughout the winter. Now she can also smile with pride as she is the proud owner of our Lily award, the same as her neighbour and another close friend.

ROSE & CALVIN McCALLUM
46 Finlayson Drive
This lovely little bungalow with a sloped interlocking stone walkway to the front door is so enchanting. The front flower bed is filled with hosta, stella dora, dill, milkweed, fennel & sea holly (to name a few) and is actually a very unique butterfly garden. Along with ornamental metal pieces, there is a butterfly house & a bird feeding station. The McCallums were away at the time, so they were quite surprised & honoured to find our Lily planted in the midst of their butterfly garden.

Our congratulations to all homeowners, who have been presented with your "Lily." We hope you display them proudly in your gardens. The Thamesford Business Association thanks you for beautifying our village.

Eva and Jessica Hatch give big smiles,
happy that their school has been saved.

Brad Cooper proudly wears a Save AJ shirt that has been
updated to celebrate the victory of the school remaining
open. A celebration was held at Brunny's in Thamesford.

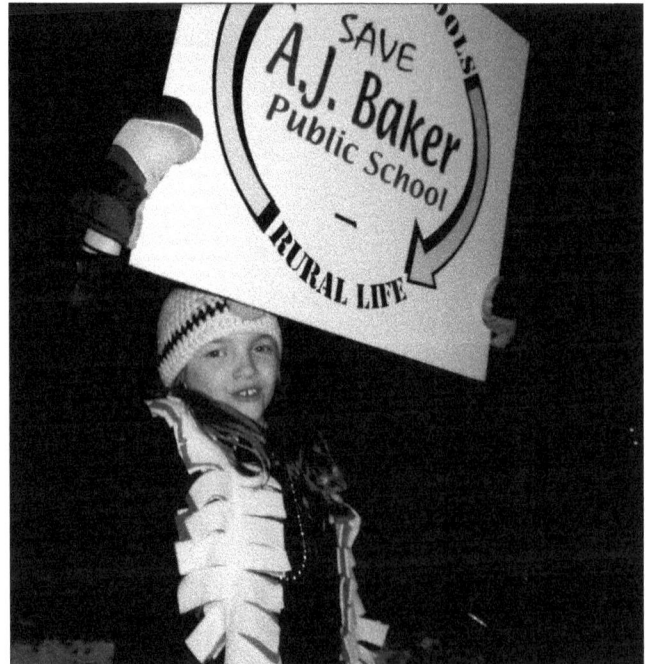

Jessica Hatch holds up a Save AJ sign

KINTORE
Save(d) AJ Baker School

Congratulations Kintore and area, we have DONE IT. They said it couldn't be done. They said every school closes that's picked for closure. They said we were doomed. They were wrong! What better lesson can a school and its community teach its children? Hard work, perseverance and a good cause can be won! The Save AJ Baker Committee thanks Kintore, Thamesford & Embro from the bottom of our hearts. What a great rural family we have! Long Live AJ Baker School!

On October 14, after almost two years of hard work, residents from all three of Zorra's school communities successfully saved A.J. Baker P.S. from closure by the Thames Valley District School Board Administration. Though many people in the larger TVDSB community thought the school was doomed to be closed, not only was it kept open, but it was a done so by an unanimous vote. The Board also took the unprecedented step of writing to the Ministry of Education to express their frustration with a system that would force them to even consider such a closure. A.J. Baker doesn't have declining enrolment and operates "in the black" for the TVDSB. Rural communities may not be "growth" communities, but we ARE growth communities: we grow food, and farmers deserve schools for their children.

A picture taken during the Save AJ campaign.
From left: Councillor Jim Verwer; Alex Steele, Daniel West,
Marcus Ryan and Henriette MacArthur.
Photos provided by Cathy West

Kintore local wins 2014 Provincial Duathlon Championship held at Lakeside

Oxford County's Scott Finch wins the 2014 Provincial Long Distance Duathlon Championship right in his backyard.

Duathletes from around Ontario descended on Lakeside on September 13, 2014 to compete for the Ontario Long Distance Duathlon Championship.

The provincial championship race brought together one of the strongest fields for a race during the 2014 season. 41 brave souls stepped up to the line in chilly temperatures, ready to take on a hilly and rough 10km run course, before battling the hills and wind for 40km on the bike, then returning for one final 5km loop of the run course.

Scott Finch of Kintore led the first 10 km run in 38:13, rode the 40 km bike course in 1:03:43 and finished with a 5 km run time of 21:13 to claim the overall victory in 2:04:24. Daryl Flacks from Windsor took second place in 2:07:00 and Etobicoke's Andrew McLeod was the third place finisher with a time of 2:08:22.

The championship has been held elsewhere in Ontario but the fact that it was being held this year in Lakeside was exciting for Finch. "It's amazing how time flies. This year marked the 10 year anniversary of my first duathlon at Lakeside, and the 12 year anniversary of my first multisport competition at this beautiful venue. So what would possess anyone to do the same race, over and over, year after year? "While I love the course, the answer is simply that the start line is exactly 8km from my front door. I train here year round. How cool is that?"

Anytime you win a championship is big accomplishment but winning it so close to home makes the training and hard work that much more rewarding. "It was great having some of the province's best duathlates competing on my home course. It was a great day for racing and I am thankful I was able to take the provincial title," said Finch.

2014 LAKESIDE RESULTS
MEN'S PROVINCIAL
DUATHLON CHAMPIONSHIP
1. Scott Finch ....(M40-49) 2:04:24
2. Daryl Flacks........................(M40-49) 2:07:01
3. Andrew McLeod..................(M40-49) 2:08:22
4. Grahame Rivers ....(M30-39) 2:10:13
5. Darren Cooney....................(M30-39) 2:10:14

WOMEN'S PROVINCIAL
DUATHLON CHAMPIONSHIP
1. Shelley O'Bright....................(F40-49) 2:27:59
2. Christine Richardson ....(F40-49) 2:33:40
3. Renee Hartford ....(F50-59) 2:37:08
4. Wendy Holyday ....(F40-49) 2:43:14
5. Alexandra Bade ....(F30-39) 2:46:28

Kintore Church 100th Anniversary

2014 marked the 100th year Anniversary of the Kintore Church building. Kintore Chalmers United Church has deep roots dating back to the 1870s. The present church building, built in 1914, was the last of at least four buildings used for Christian worship in and around Kintore. The current Chalmers United Church was originally built as a Presbyterian church.

To celebrate the 100th year anniversary a Reunion Concert was held Saturday, September 27, 2014 and a 100th Anniversary Service was held the following day. Speakers at the service included Mayor Margaret Lupton, Rev. Beth Chapman, George Quinn, and Gail Kavelman.

The Saturday night reunion concert featured fun, music and nostalgia. Rev. Doug Peck presided as MC to a SOLD-OUT house! A trip down memory lane was had through a slide show of times gone by and a celebration of the church's musical heritage. Many former stars returned to share their talents.

The church is currently still an active part of the Kintore community. Beyond its regular duties as a house of worship it also provides a place for community activities such as Knitting and More, Parent/Child Drop-in, VON exercise for seniors and other community events.

100TH
Anniversary
CHALMERS UNITED CHURCH - KINTORE
1914 - 2014

CELEBRATING OUR PAST
embracing our future

Kintore 1910 and 1988

THE WAY WE WERE

THEN The Kintore General Store and post office is shown in this postcard, circa 1910, from the collection of Don Whetstone of London.

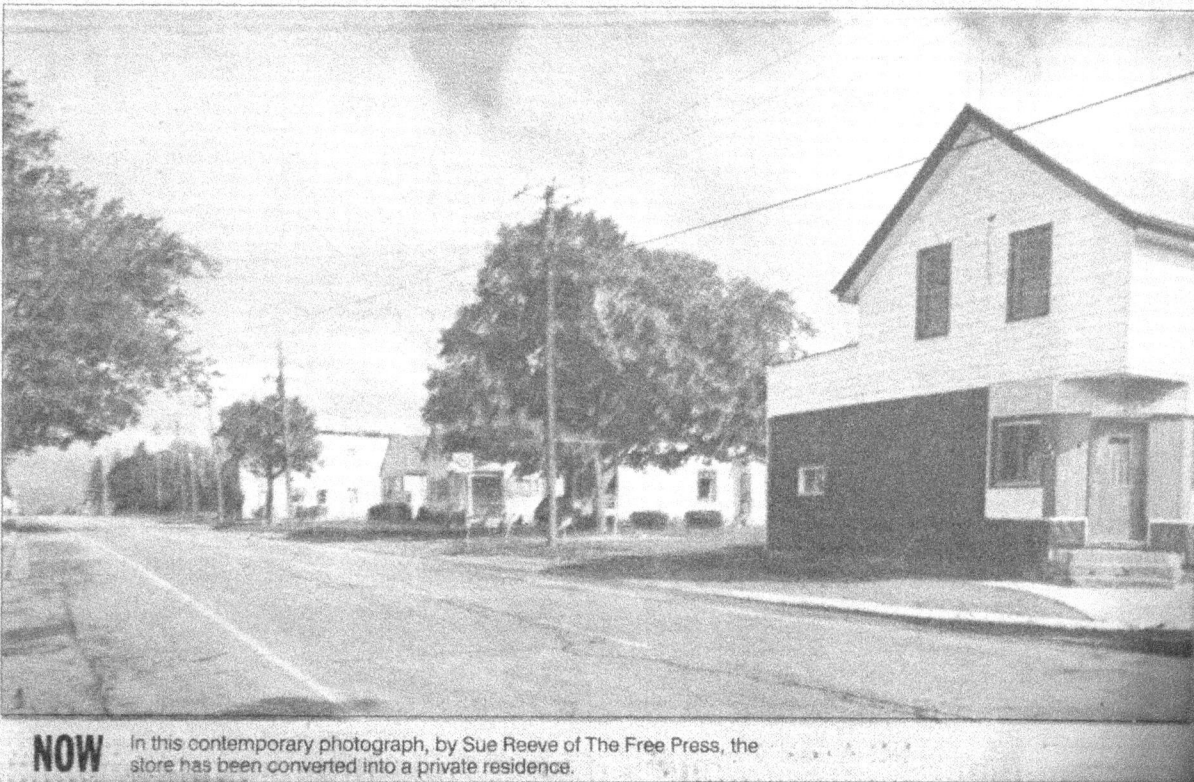

NOW In this contemporary photograph, by Sue Reeve of The Free Press, the store has been converted into a private residence.

Aerial view of Lakeside 1977

THE C.P.R. ALSO HAD PROBLEMS as the engine and several cars jumped the track on the Woodstock-St. Marys line in West Zorra Township about three miles east of Lakeside last Monday. Ice was blamed for the mishap. The picture above was taken Tuesday afternoon. The recovery train, complete with crane, may be seen in the background. The J.A. cameraman could sympathize with the C.P.R. work crew as the firm's van had gently slid into a snow-bank along the adjoining road a few minutes before this picture was taken. Our recovery job was fortunately not as complicated as that facing the men in the scene above.

From February 2, 1971

LAKESIDE

Arriving in Style:
Campbell boys ride to school on a fire truck

Staff and students of AJ Baker Public School greet the Campbell brothers as they arrive to school on a Zorra fire truck.

It was an exciting morning for Nick and Nate Campbell on Monday October 5, 2015.

Zorra Fire and Emergency Services provided a "Ride to School in a Fire Truck" for the Campbell boys. The family had purchased the ride during silent auction fundraiser held during AJ Baker Public School's Fun Fair held last spring.

Paul Mitchell, Uniondale District Fire Chief, picked up the two boys just before 9 a.m. They outfitted them with fire helmets, coats and a pager before heading to AJ Baker Public School. The entire school was waiting in the front yard of the school to greet the fire truck as it pulled up to drop the boys off for the day.

The ride also helped kick off the beginning of Fire Prevention Week.

Christ Church, Lakeside

Christ Church Anglican Lakeside is still part of the Parish of The Thames (St. John's in Thamesford, St. George's in Thorndale, and St. Luke's in Crumlin) but is now a Chapel of Ease. This means there are no regular services and we are in actuality restricted to 6 services a year.

The parishioners who still remain are responsible for maintaining the building and the grounds but must resort to outside fund raising and donations to pay expenses. As the Church Hall is a separate building, the parishioners are able to use it for meetings and some bible study but no worship services.

The cemetery is a separate entity and is managed by a small appointed group who rely on the collection from the Decoration Sunday Service (one of the six services) and the sale of grave plots to maintain the grounds.

The remaining parishioners are trying to meet at 1:00pm on Sundays to conduct an open discussion on a variety of topics and what the Holy Word may have to say to us on these topics. It is a very informal session with refreshments and snacks being enjoyed while the thoughts are shared.

Award of Bravery

Pictured are Eli Day, Tyler Fowler, Governor-General David Johnston and Dion Lefebvre
Photo taken by Sgt. Ronald Duchesne, Rideau Hall

In April 2012, Eli Day was one of three people who pulled four people from their burning vehicles following a violent head-on collision near Wandering River, Alberta. Despite rapidly spreading fire, all victims were extricated. Sadly, several occupants of both vehicles did not survive.

Eli received the Government of Canada Medal of Bravery in October 2014 at a ceremony held at Rideau Hall, Ottawa. The award was presented by His Excellency the Right Honourable David Johnston, Governor General of Canada. The Medal of Bravery was created in 1972 to recognize people who risked their lives to try to save or protect the lives of others. It recognizes acts of bravery in hazardous circumstances.

Eli is the son of Cathy Segeren and Keith Day of Lakeside and now resides in Fawcett, Alberta with his family - Tara McKay and their children Maddox, Wyatt and Aria.

World Waterski Competitor

Bill Tallman of Lakeside competed as one of 24 Team Canada athletes in the Senior World Waterski Championships October 2014 held in Groveland, Florida.

There were skiers from 33 countries and Bill placed 12th in the slalom event. Bill won 17 Ontario Championships and in the eight years previous to this event, Bill held five National titles. Sadly, at the age of 70, Bill passed away November 12, 2015.

Bill at the World Championships Orlando Florida - October 2014

Lakeside 1910 and 1989

THE LONDON FREE PRESS ○ JANUARY 7, 1989

THE WAY WE WERE
PAGE SEVENTEEN

St. View Lakeside ont

THEN King Street in Lakeside is shown in this postcard, circa 1910, from the collection of Don Whetstone of London.

NOW In this contemporary photograph, by Sue Reeve of The Free Press, the same westerly view from Brook Street is shown.

Organic ONEder

Tim and Julie started an organic food distribution business in 2013 called Organic ONEder, and the business has since grown to include several holistic practices. Julie is a certified Holistic Practitioner specializing in Foot Reflexology. Also offered is Therapeutic Touch, Ear Candling, and Foot Detox Cleanses.

Tim is currently engaged in a two year course to become a Registered Holistic Nutritionist (RHN). He will be certified in the fall of 2017. They have launched an official website at www.organiconeder.com where product lists are posted and services explained. They can also be reached at 519-349-2853. These side careers keep them both very busy, but they are passionate about living a healthy lifestyle, and enjoy passing on all of the things they have learned to those who are interested.

Lakeside Yoga

In 2013, Karen Zehnal opened the first yoga studio in the village of Lakeside, offering individual and small group classes in yoga and meditation. The Zehn Loft is located at 287 Mank Street and overlooks Lake Sunova and Betty Mank Park. For more information about classes and events, go to www.zehnconnection.ca or email karen@zehnconnection.ca.

Hensall District Co-Operative

Hensall District Co-Operative is located just east of Lakeside at the corner of Line 27 and Road 92. This is a farmer-owned agri-business which dries and stores many kinds of crops. It was purchased from Clarence and Sharon in July 1997 by Elaine and Gary Yantzi. At that time the dryer capacity was 400 bu/hour and storage was 150,000 bushels. Over the years the drying capacity was increased to 2000 bu/hour and the storage increased to 1.1 million bushels. It was purchased by Hensall District Co-Op in August 2014.

HARRINGTON

Harrington Outdoor Rink

Volunteers in Harrington building outdoor skating rink on the baseball diamond – winter 2015.

UNIONDALE

Uniondale Firefighters BBQ

Uniondale Firefighters Chicken BBQ September 10, 2015 4:30-7:30 at Browns Corners - church shed. Adults $15 (1/2 chicken), 6-12 $7 (1/4) chicken, 5 and under no charge. Takeout available.

Preparation for the event

www.heroes of zorra.ca

Heroes of Zorra Website Moving Forward

By Shirley McCall-Hanlon

Thanks to the efforts of many local and area residents and families far away, the Heroes Of Zorra (HOZ) web site has grown immensely since it was launched in August 2013. Many pictures and additional information has been added to numerous veterans. The elementary school children across the Township of Zorra have been encouraged to learn more about our "Heroes" by participating in the 2014 contest where school grades were divided and created collages, pamphlets, brochures and videos based on the information they learned from this site. In 2015 an old-fashioned Spelling Bee was held and all elementary children across Zorra were eligible to enter. All words used were gleaned from the site. Both contests were a success. We encourage all who are reading this to share the information with family and friends and if you happen to have more information on a particular veteran, please contact us via the web site www.heroesofzorra.ca

For those of you waiting to see the veterans who served from the former Township of North Oxford, these will be available early in January 2016, if not sooner. Again, we know there will be some of you who can help us to document more information on these individuals too. Please check back to the site often.

Since the site was launched we have had more information added on the following individuals:

The Honorable James Sutherland
Guy John Goodhand
Neil Eastman Goodhand
Gordon M.R. Goodhand
John Gates
Edward Robert Hill
Robert Alvin McDonald
William Lowrie Hill
Cecil William Kerr
Howard Innes
Jason Zilke
Daniel Munroe
William Munroe
John Ross MacKay
George Alexander Gordon
Harris Wesley (Harry) Masters
Russell Master, Helen Masters
Ward Ralph Waddle
Frances Walton
Todd Whetstone
Ralph Webb
Murray Tizzard
William John Robertshaw
Donald A. Olson Jr.
William Wallace Murray
George Alexander Murray
Robert Murray McDonald
Calvin McKay McIntosh
William Stanley Heal
George Jackson
Clarence Eckert Kalbfleisch
F.A. Hammett
John Ransom Gates
Gordon Gibb
Gordon Frost
Charles Daynes
Donald Carey
Jean Burgess Atkinson
Quincey Randolph Sutherland
Frank Higgins
John Gordon (Gordon) McCall
Donald Burns (Burns) McCall
Edward Robert Hill
John Allen McKay
James Slater
Donald Gard
George Gard
William Andrew (Tim) McDonald
Benjamin Franklin Youngs
Elsie Gertrude Ross
James Gordon (Jamie) Ross
George Osborne MacKenzie
Alfred Edwin McKay
John Alvin McKay
Alex W. McKay
Alex McCorquodale
Daniel Osker Sutherland
Daniel Quinn
David William Calvert
Daniel Quinn Calvert
Kenneth McGirr
Frank McGirr, Alfred Jenkins
Wilbert Russell Cove
Charles Milton Agar
Elgin Cyrus Hutchison
Arthur Thomas Hutchison.

Military   Military   Military   Military   Military

Heroes of Zorra

Front row: Lannie Schurman, (Runner Up - Gr 5 and under), Finn Stewart (Winner of Gr 5 and under), Sydney Turvey (Winner of Gr 6-8) and Katie Schurman (runner up of Gr 6-8).
Back row: participants Ryan Vandersar, Ava Wilks, Nathan Bean and Jacob Vandersar.

HEROES OF ZORRA
HONORING OUR MILITARY

HOME HISTORY VETERANS STORIES DONORS YOUTH CONTACT US

Recognizing the many individuals from the Township of Zorra Ontario, who have served our country from the 1860's to the present day.

HEROES OF ZORRA SPELLING BEE

On November 22, 2015 the Heroes Of Zorra committee held a Spelling Bee for all elementary school students across the Township of Zorra at the Royal Canadian Legion in Embro. The words given to the students were all to be found on the Heroes Of Zorra web site. Two divisions were offered - Grade 5 & under and Grades 6, 7, 8. The winner in each division received $100 and the runner-up $75. Every contestant was presented with a Heroes Of Zorra medal by committee member Doris McCall. Eight young people signed up for this first ever event. Each & every one was a winner. Parents, grandparents & friends were so proud of their efforts. Our Bee Master (that is the person who gives the word to the students & uses that word in a sentence) was very capably handled by Scott Naisbit. Our judges were Mayor Margaret Lupton & Roy Youngs and the timekeepers were Shirley Zilke & John Milner. MC for the event was Shirley McCall-Hanlon. The enthusiastic community spirit demonstrated at this event was once again exemplary within the Township of Zorra.

MILITARY

Pre Fenian Raids

James Sutherland was born about 1786. He died April 11, 1873 and was buried in the North Embro Cemetery.

Obituary from the Woodstock Weekly Review April 18, 1873:

SUTHERLAND - In West Zorra, on the 11th inst.: James Sutherland, (pensioner) in the 87th year of his age. Deceased was a British soldier for 23 years, and served in the 79th Cameronian Highlander regiment. He fought with Wellington at Waterloo in 1815, for which service he received a silver medal, bearing an insignia of the times. He also received a silver medal for good conduct - never having been once in the guard house. Besides the above medals, he held one presented by Queen Victoria in 1848, for services rendered in six foreign battles, viz: - "Toulouse", "Nive", "Nivelle". "Pyrenees", "Salamanca", and "Fuentes D'Onor". The medals are now in the hands of his children. Deceased was among the oldest settlers having been located in this Township for upwards of 37 years; during which time he gained many friends, and was highly respected by all who knew him. His remains were interred in the cemetery, here, on Monday. The funeral was largely attended.

Clarence B. Martin

World War I

Baker, Henry (1896-1983) was born in Harrington West but was raised on Lot 35, Concession 1. His father was John Baker; his mother, Jennie (Reid, Baker) Hewitt. Henry was a student at the Stratford Teacher's College before he enlisted June 12,1916.

Chandler, Pte. Wentworth (Jan. 8, 1889-April 22, 1922) was born in Lakeside to Sarah (Vansichte) and John Chandler. At the time he enlisted he was living in Tavistock and had served for a year with Grey's Horse. He served with the 1st Canadian Infantry Battalion. He died at Queen Alexandra Sanatorium of tuberculosis in 1922.

Martin, Benjamin Clarence #7272638 (1887-1963) was born at Kintore to Joseph H. and Mary Elizabeth (nee Cooper) Martin. Clarence joined the 110th (Perth) Canadian Infantry Battalion on March 4, 1916. He arrived in France April 4, 1917 with twenty-four reinforcements to the 58th Battalion for the Battle of Vimy Ridge. On April 11th while drawing enemy fire in no-man's-land he suffered a serious bullet wound, causing a compound fracture of his right femur. After eight hours he was able to crawl back to his lines, but wasn't evacuated for treatment until the following morning. He spent the remainder of the war in hospital, not being discharged from the army until March 9, 1920. On April 26, 1923 he married Gladys Rene Mossey. They farmed 190 acres on the Mitchell Road near Science Hill, Blanchard Township from this time until 1941. They then bought a farm on the South Boundary of Blanchard Township, between Queen Street and James Street (now owned by the cement plant - 1958). They raised 4 children, Douglas, June, Betty, and Jack.

Upon their retirement Clarence and Gladys resided a short time in Exeter and then moved to Peel Street, St. Marys, Ontario.

Morrison, Allan Ironside #3311125 (b. 1896) was from East Nissouri and was drafted in Oct. 1917 to serve in WWI.

Morrison, G. Clive was the son of Angus and Violet Morrison of Concession 9, Lot 20 of East Zorra Township. He attended SS #10 Elmsdale Public School in West Zorra. Clive Morrison started Youth Training School, Galt on February 28, 1941 and enlisted in the Royal Canadian Air Force at #1 Manning Pool, Toronto on July 19, 1941. He received basic training in Toronto, Winnipeg and St. Thomas. From

Clive G. Morrison

March 1942 to January 1944 he was with the Eastern Coastal Command Squadron and was stationed at Gander Bay, Newfoundland, Goose Bay, Labrador and Yarmouth and Dartmouth, Nova Scotia. In January 1944 he was posted overseas to Iceland, where he spent 15 months before returning to Canada. During his time in Iceland his squadron was on Coastal Patrol work and had several successful attacks on submarines, but also had considerable loss of life and aircraft. Clive was a member of the 162nd Squadron in which Flight Lieutenant David Hornell of Mimicio was awarded the Victorian Cross posthumously, the first to earn it in the RCAF and the third Canadian. The Squadron was also awarded several DFC's and DFM's. Clive returned to Canada and was stationed at Mont Joli, Quebec until he received his discharge in Toronto on September 27, 1945.

World War II

Baker, Terence A. (Terry) enlisted in February 1940 and received his preliminary training at Camp Borden. He was sent overseas later in 1940 and received further training at Camp Bognor Regis in England and commando training in Scotland. He was in the Sicilian invasion early in the fall of 1943 and served in Germany, Belgium and Holland. Terry met his future wife, Brigid Halls,

early in the war at Camp Bognor Regis. They were married on May 28, 1945 prior to both of them being discharged. Early in the spring of 1946 they purchased the one hundred acre farm of R.M. Matheson at Lot 24, Concession 9 of East Zorra. In 1958 they moved to Lot 30, Concession 6 of West Zorra. He and Breda raised 4 children - Deirdre, Michale, Gregory and David.

Baker, William Earl was born in West Zorra Township, the son of William Lyle Baker and Clara Marlborough Ford. He attended S.S. #7 (Wadland's) public school in West Zorra along with siblings Robert John, Alan Joseph, Stuart Wesley, Beatrice Louise, Vera Luella and Edna Rachel. On December 4, 1942 he enlisted in London, Ontario and received his training at Debert Camp, Nova Scotia and Chatham, New Brunswick. He served in England and earned the Canadian

William Earl Baker

Volunteer Service Medal and Clasp. Earl was also a Past President of Royal Canadian Legion, Memorial Branch 518, Tavistock, Ontario.

Evans, Evelyn William Barnabus (known throughout West Zorra as Barney) was born in Harecroft, Orpington, Kent, England on June 11, 1922. He enlisted with the Royal Air Force, Squadron 102. In January of 1944 he was shot down near Berlin. Barney emigrated to Canada in 1962 and operated a business named Zorra Farms. He passed away on August 29, 1987 and is buried in Maitland Cemetery, Goderich.

Barney Evans

Joan Evans

Evans, Joan Cameron (nee Wilson) was the wife of Evelyn William Barnabus (Barney) Evans who also served in World War 11. Joan and Barney raised four children - Rosalind, Rupert, Joene and Elizabeth. Joan passed away on January 22, 2015 and is buried with her husband in Maitland Cemetery, Goderich, Ontario.

Gleason, Arnold (1921- Dec. 4, 2013) son of Charles (Chad) and Verna Gleason of East Nissouri enlisted with the Royal Canadian Air Force serving with 422 Squadron Coastal Command. Arnold and his wife Molly are parents to Arlene and John. He is buried at Mt. Pleasant Cemetery in London, Ontario.

Arnold Gleason

John "Forbes" Green is on the left

Green, John "Forbes" was born April 21, 1917 in Perth County. Forbes served his country in WWII. In June 1945 he married Helen McKay of Harrington, and together they farmed the family farm at Fairview. Forbes and Helen raised 3 sons, Jim, Ken and Doug. Forbes died February 6, 2010 and is buried in Harrington West Presbyterian Church Cemetery. Helen is currently living at Hamlet Estates, in Stratford.

Halls, Breda of Hounslow, Middlesex, England joined the Women's Auxiliary Air Force in 1941. She received her basic training at Gloucester and her training as a pay clerk at Penarth, South Wales. She served on Royal Air Force stations on Thorney Island near Portsmouth, Stranraer, Scotland, Halton in Buckinghamshire and Redding, England. She met her future husband Terence Baker at Camp Bognor Regis early in the war and they were married May 28, 1945. Mrs. Baker came to Canada aboard the Queen Mary in May 1946, arriving in Halifax on their first wedding anniversary. She and Terry raised 4 children - Deirdre, Michale, Gregory and David.

Terry and Breda Baker's tombstone

Hutchison, Joseph Edward (Lorne) was the son of Edward and Violet (nee Bean) Hutchison and was born on December 7, 1914 in West Zorra Township. He was the brother of Elgin and Arthur. After returning from service Lorne moved to Vancouver, British Columbia.

Joseph Edward Hutchinson

MacDougald, Colin was born in August of 1917. Colin and his wife Mildred were married at Cromarty (Perth County) on January 20, 1937. In November of 1938 Colin and Mildred took over the store in Harrington. They rented it from Minnie Clark until they purchased it in 1944. Colin was postmaster and also had an egg route and grading station at the store from 1938-1958. While Colin was in the armed forces for about 2 1/2 years Mildred was the acting postmaster. They later retired to Bracebridge.

McGirr, Sergeant Raymond William son of George and Jean (nee MacArthur) McGirr of east half Lot 28 Con 9, East Nissouri Township enlisted into the Royal Canadian Air Force in 1942 and served during World War II. When the war was over Raymond remained in the Military Service. He married Emmy Lou Shields and together they raised a family of 2 daughters and 1 son - Rebecca, William and Jocelyn. After retiring from the Military in 1969, he then worked on the Dew Line until 1985. Raymond and Emmy Lou then retired to Gabriola Island, British Columbia where they currently reside in July 2015.

Raymond William McGirr

McGirr, Gunner Russell Norman (1921-1961) was the son of George and Jean (nee McArthur) McGirr of east half Lot 28 Con 9, East Nissouri Township. He served from 1944. Following the war he married Elizabeth (Bette) Wolsey and together they raised three daughters, Margaret, Janet and Peggy.

Montgomery, Harry Ferguson lived in the Braemar area of Zorra and served as a Lance Corporal in the Royal Canadian Army Service Corps. He was awarded the RCASC medal as noted per Canada Gazette dated March 9, 1946. Harry's name was found on a list of community veterans.

Parker, John Wilfred (Jack) was born on December 14, 1913 in Ingersoll, Ontario. He was a Private during WWII.

Parker, Flight Sergeant Ralph Budd was born in West Zorra a son of Thomas William and Edna May (nee Phillips) Parker. He went to school up to grade three there and then went to Victory Memorial School and Ingersoll Collegiate Institute in Ingersoll. In 1928 he moved to Ingersoll. He remembers walking to Ingersoll, driving cattle. He lived with Jim Fergusson who was Mayor of Ingersoll in the 1930's.

In 1940 he married Beatrice Kugler of Southampton. In 1943 Ralph enlisted in the Royal Canadian Air Force. After basic training in Toronto, he took an advanced course at Queen's University in Kingston and then with Mont-Joli in Quebec, at an air gunnery school.

After graduation from the gunnery school he chose to stay on as an instructor so was sent to take the training course at Belleville. Ralph taught air gunnery at Mont-Joli until January 1, 1945 when he was posted to Boundary Bay, B.C. At Abbotsford, B.C. they got together a crew - pilot, co-pilot, navigator, air gunners, radio operator. Ralph was the tail gunner on a Liberator aircraft.

Ralph Budd Parker & family

Ralph had a bad moment when a plane he was in belly landed at Mont-Joli. "There's an unwritten rule that you never let a plane bounce three times. Well, ours did and the wheels went right up through the wings".

He went back to Mont-Joli to teach turrets and hydraulics. Ralph was actually posted overseas after VE Day. He was posted to Bournemouth, England and slated to go to India. However, the A Bomb was dropped. Sent back home, the Flight Sergeant landed on New York Harbour on February 5, 1946, saw the Statue of Liberty for the first time and froze his toes.

Back home, Dr. Harry Furlong advised him that he knew of a farm that was available at a reasonable price. "It was in bad shape, but we fixed it up and made it home. My son Tom has it today."

Ralph and Beatrice raised four children: Tom, Lois, Patricia and Virginia. He is a Past President of Branch 119 Royal Canadian Legion and today, in 2013 resides in Ingersoll, Ontario.

Schaefer, George A. was the son of Mr. & Mrs. Alfred Schaefer who lived on Thames Street in Embro. He served his country in WW11. George was with the Eighth Army when he was wounded in action on January 18, 194_. The extent of his injuries were not known.

George A. Schaefer

Varnum, Arthur RCAF # R155041 (1924-1990) was born in Edmonton. He took basic training in Lethbridge, Edmonton, Alberta as a Navigator and Bomb Aimer. After going overseas he was at Wigtown, Scotland and with Squadron 298, Terrant Preston, Dorset, England. He flew in Sterling and Halifax aircraft and remained in England until the end of the war. Upon returning to Canada he went to the Ontario College of Pharmacy in Toronto and graduated in 1951. He worked for a few drug stores in London before coming to Thamesford and opening his own business called Varnum Drug Store. He worked there until he retired in 1988. Upon retiring he and his wife Isabell went to the Wartime Aircrew Re-Union in Winnipeg, Manitoba. He is buried at Zion Seventh Line Cemetery.

Youngs, William Alonzo was born on January 12, 1923. He was the son of John Egbert and Margaretta (nee McDonald) Youngs of West Zorra. He enlisted in the Royal Canadian Air Force. He was killed in action in Germany on July 18, 1944 and is commemorated at Baron on Surmur, France (near Paris).

William Alonzo Youngs

Korean War

MacKay, Murray, was the son of Stanley and Nina (nee Saul) of Thamesford. He was born in Thamesford, Ontario on February 13, 1934 and enlisted with the Royal Canadian Navy. Murray was very proud of the fact that at one time he was the youngest Petty Officer in all of Canada. He served on several ships as an Electrician's Mate from 1952-1957. Those ships were the HMCS Prevost, HMCS Cornwallis, HMCS Stadacona, HMCS Magnificent (Aircraft Carrier) and the HMCS Quebec which was a cruiser. On August 11, 1957 he married Marilyn Caldwell and they resided for many years on the MacKay family homestead at Lot 14 and part Lot 13 Concession 2 of West Zorra Township, Oxford County, Ontario, Canada. They raised four children - Heather, Scott, Karen and Jamie.

The Dumbells

The Dumbells, a group of soldier-entertainers who made life easier for Canadian troops on the Western front during the First World War, would be a nearly forgotten piece of history if not for Jason Wilson. The Toronto musician is reviving the comedy and music act The Dumbells took from the battlefield to vaudeville in a performance. His show, Soldiers of Song, has been performed across Canada. He's so passionate about the group that he's also written a book about them. Wilson believes The Dumbells founded a great tradition of Canadian comedy that extends to groups like Wayne and Shuster and Kids in the Hall.

The Dumbells went to Broadway in the 1920s. (Private collections of John McLaren and Stephen Plunkett.) The Dumbells poked fun at authority with their comedy and funny songs, providing Canadian soldiers a couple of hours of relief from the fighting in Europe during the First World War.

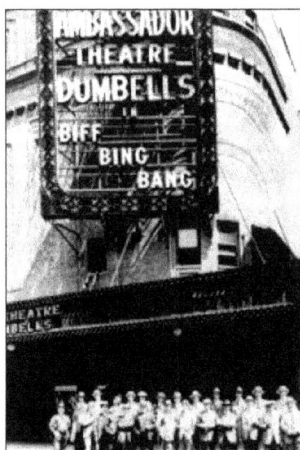
The Dumbells went to Broadway in the 1920s.

"The Dumbells were allowed to make fun of almost everything, though not everything," Wilson said in an interview with CBC's Deana Sumanac. "One of those things was superior officers, who turned their cheek and said 'This is all in the interest of morale and trying to keep this show going and doing our best.' They were able to make fun of death. They were able to make fun of the war itself." According to Wilson, only poison gas and shellshock were out of bounds in their skewering of the military and its systems.

Formed in 1917 by members of the Canadian army's Third Division, the troupe was named for the red dumbbell in the division's emblem. The group's job was to bolster morale among soldiers with live "concert parties" featuring irreverent humour. After the war, The Dumbells toured Canada, had a run in London's West End and scored a hit on Broadway when vaudeville was still going strong.

Capt. Mert Plunkett, founder of The Dumbells, was a composer and comic genius.

The original Dumbells disbanded in 1932, but reunited for concerts in 1939 and 1955. Wilson believes the Canadian talent for sketch comedy also began with the Dumbells, who — as an all-male troupe — dressed some of its actors in women's clothing for certain roles.

OXFORD COUNTY MUSEUM SCHOOL
Preserving Ontario's Educational Heritage

A visit to the Oxford County Museum School is like embarking on a personal journey through local history. A reminder of Ontario's educational heritage, the Museum School provides students, educators, and the general public a unique, hands-on experience. The Museum School has recently returned to its original name, the Oxford County Museum School. This reflects its mandate of collecting educational material from Oxford County.

The Museum School is also pleased to announce its new location. We have been welcomed to the Ingersoll Cheese and Agricultural Museum, where we have taken up residence on the site in a building that we have begun to turn into a replica of a rural schoolhouse. Our exhibits, the educational programs, and the activities have begun, including Canadiana Challenge. Our extensive collection including the archives is housed at the Town of Ingersoll Town Hall, located at 130 Oxford St.

Our original location, the Thames Valley Museum School, was a Baronial-styled, two-room, red brick schoolhouse was constructed in 1905. Formerly known as S.S. #3 North Norwich, this elaborately designed structure was the fourth school built in the community and faced south to direct maximum sunlight across students' desks. After serving the community faithfully for decades, modernization signaled the school's closure. One and two-room schoolhouses across rural Ontario suffered a similar fate in the 1960s, as centralized

facilities, school bussing, and larger structures became the norm. In 1976, through the efforts of the Oxford County Elementary Principals' Association and the former Oxford County Board of Education, a new chapter was written for S.S. #3.

Created on the belief that knowledge and awareness of the past are important to understand the present and to plan for the future, the Museum School was charged to house and to display educational artifacts and to provide an authentic historical teaching centre for area students. Today, the not-for-profit Friends of the Oxford County Museum School is responsible for the operation of the Museum School. Its mission is to preserve, exhibit and interpret artifacts and archival material reflecting the educational history of Oxford County and Ontario. This mission continues in our new location.

Schools

S.S. No. 11 September 1898

Back row: Gordon McKenzie, Jack Gleason, Will McKenzie, Josie Whetstone, Fred Mackintee, Zedric Clipperton, Walter Gleason, Charles Harris, Albert Strubsole, Vincent Gregory.

3rd Row: Lena Bolton, Jean Darling, Marg Bossence, Maple Whetstone, Edith Gregory, Clara Whetstone, Grace Bayne, Addie Whetstone, Rubeena Gleason, Ethel Johnson, Annie Bayne, Mame Bayne (Teacher)

2nd row: Gladys McKim, Winnie McKim, Alma McKim, Bessie Mills, Ethel Gregory, Lelola Whetstone, Mary Agnes Welfare, Leman Harris, Bill Johnson, Hugh Whetstone, Hugh Harris.

Front row: Vera Clipperton, Olive Mackintee, Carrie Mackintee, Merle Clipperton, Annie Welfare, Sadie Murphy, Verna Whetstone, Minnie Whetstone, Olive Matheson, Bill Matheson

S.S. No. 11 McKims ca. 1911-12

Back row: Marion Baker, Ethel Beacham, Jean Matheson.
Middle Row: Harvey Whetstone, George Dawes, John Lotten, Merle Dawes, Eva Matheson,
Davina Cole, _____Tomlinson.
Front Row: Ackland Baker, Jack Tomlinson, Annie Lotten, John Baker, and Harry Snell

McKims P.S. S.S. No. 11 Circa 1915

A photograph of a day in life of a classroom in 1915.

Notice the hand drawn map of Oxford county on the wall.

The iron and wood work on the desks is impressive as well.

Back row: Albert Dawes, Harold McLarkey, Jack Thomlinson, _____, Ackland Baker, Harry Snell, John Baker
Front row: Stanley Pearson, Helen McKim, _____, Annie Lotten, Mabel Tomlinson, _____

S.S. No. 3 Browns 1930

Back Row: Douglas Conn, Fred Arthur, Perry McDonald, Harry Muir
Row#3: Marie McDonald, Viola Elliott, Joyce Burgess, Irene Pearson, Robert Burgess
Row #2: Don Purdie, Dorothy Near, Verne McDonald, Marjorie Ledmen, Ada Arthur
Front Row: Grant Elliott, Ernva MacDonald, Alice Ledman, Audrey Vanatter, Austin Vanatter

S.S. No. 6 Reunion held 1937

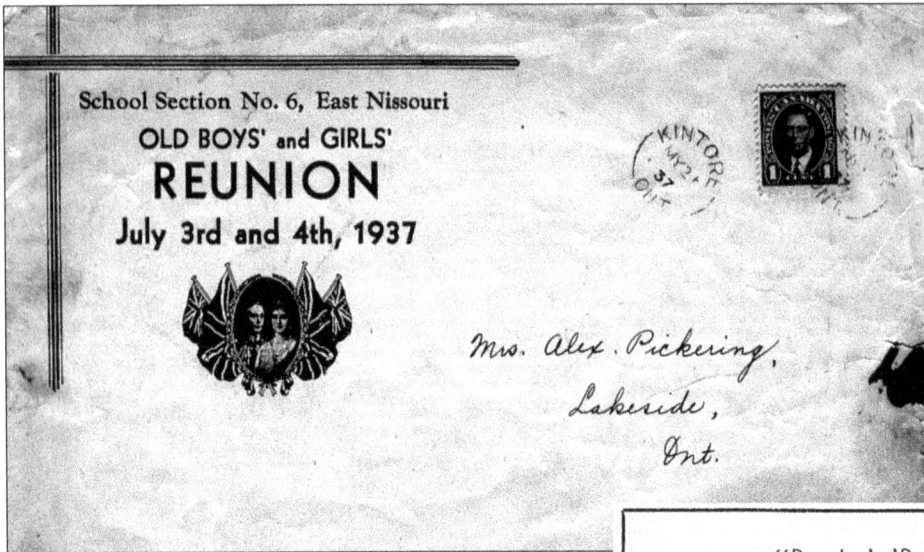

School Section No. 6, East Nissouri

OLD BOYS' and GIRLS'

REUNION

July 3rd and 4th, 1937

Mrs. Alex. Pickering,
Lakeside,
Ont.

*SS # 6 Reunion
was held July 3rd and 4th, 1937 in Kintore.*

Over 400 people attended the weekend event.

*Pictures of the classes represented at the reunion
can be found on page 290 and 291
of the East Zorra History Book.*

*Above is a picture of the envelope
from the invitation that was mailed out
inviting guests to the reunion.*

*To the right is a photo of a page
from the school reunion.
This is the most accurate list of teachers.*

"Readin' 'Ritin' and 'Rithmatic, Taught to the Tune of the Hickory Stick."

Wielded by the following Teachers

1853-54	John Talon
1855	William Thomas
1856-57	Thomas Tier
1857	Annie Tier
1858	Fitzgerald Sutherland
1859-60	Mary J. Service
1861-62	Mary Adams
1862-63	John Hay
1863	Andrew Glendenning
1863-64	John Ross
1865-67	James Morrison
1868	Robert Irvin
1869-72	Donald Morrison
1873	James Slater
1874	George MacPherson
1875-77	Christena MacKay
1878	Christena Howes
1879-82	Maggie L. Ross
1883	Frank Uren
1883	Duncan Hargreaves
1884-85	Jas. W. Moyer
1886-87	Agnes Stainton
1888-89	William W. Day
1890	Alex Ferguson
1891-92	James A. Young
1893-95	Alice Furse
1896-98	Minnie S. Molland
1899-1900	H. C. Ross
1900-01	Fred C. Thornton
1902-05	Mary E. Ireton
1906-08	Maggie Smith
1909	Serena Atkinson
1909-12	Florence G. Farrier
1912-18	Jean K. Mair
1918-19	Theresa Switzer
1919-22	Mary Core
1922-23	Marion Hooper
1923-27	Agnes McNair
1927-29	Helen Oliver
1929-31	Marion Calder
1931-36	Elma B. Wardell
1936-37	Heleen McKay

S.S. No. 7 Wadland's School 1938-1939

1938 - 39   Teacher   Alice   Gleason

Back Row - Donnie Manson, Mac MacLeod, Marion Lindsay, Helen Smith, Vic Lindsay, Jack Cooper.
Row 2 - Albert Smith, Doris Smith, John MacLeod, Edna Baker, Pearl Walters. Allan Baker
Row 3 - Audrey Horman, Betty Green, Stuart Baker, Netta Smith, Margaret Green, Margaret
Front - Charlie Horman, John Innes, Bill Lindsay, Bob Walters.

S.S. No. 4 Uniondale P.S. May 1938

Back row: Arlis Robbins, Jean Richardson, Wilma Wakem, Rumble (Teacher), Nellie Mae Smith, Doris Elliott, Annie Bain
3rd Row: Norman Hutton, Glenna Robbins, Norma Robbins, Wonetta Smith, Ivan Smith, Norman Peckam
2nd row: Calvin Richardson, Mac Smith, Don King, _____, Bill Smith, Jack Richardson
Front row: Bryant Smith, ___ Peckham, ____ Peckham, Murray Kingdon

S.S. No. 11 McKims P.S. 1941

Teacher: Alice Gleason Back row: Bill Langdon, Thelma Beacham, Jim Langdon, Evelyn Shrubsole, Ivan Beacham,
Joyce Martin, Ken Cole, Mary Chandler, Elizabeth Harris, Ruth Gregory, Ray Dawes, Jean Harris
Front Row: Ron Allen, May Cole, Ron Beacham, Jean Langdon, Ken Kittmer, Bob Dawes, Ken Harris,
Bob Harris, Mary Harris, Jack Kittmer, Margret Harris

S.S. No. 11 McKims P.S. 1942

McKims' students posing at the flowerbeds.

Jack Kittmer, May Cole, Jean Langdon with Bob Daves and Ken Kittmer sitting in front

S.S. No. 11 McKims P.S. 1945

Back row: Jim Leatham (teacher), Ken Kittmer, Ron Beacham, Bob Harris, Mary Harris, May Cole, Mary Wells
Middle Row: Lois Gregory, Jean Langdon, Jack Kittmer, Bernie Beacham, Stewart McKenzie, Jim Kittmer
Front Row: Ruth Harris, Kathleen Gregory, Patsy Kittmer, Bob Wells, Bob Kittmer

S.S. No. 10 P.S. 1946

Lakeside Public School was located towards the back of the school lot at part Lot 22 con 13. The school board had painted the white brick structure red. Mr. Denstedt, the teacher, painted the white fence around the school.

S.S. No. 11 McKims P.S. 1947-48

Back Row: Jack Kittmer, Jim Kittmer, Bernie Beacham, Una Calder (Teacher), Mary Wells
Middle Row: Margaret Baker, Ruth Harris, Patsy Kittmer, Lois Gregory
Front Row: Bob Wells, Bob Kittmer, Larry Oakes, Allan Gregory

S.S. No. 9 Holiday School 1950 Grade 8

*Back Row:
Robert McDonald,
Hugh Hossack,
Maybelle Hossack,
Noreen Hossack,
Teacher: Mr. Pratt*

*Front Row:
Sharon Moore,
Sharon Hossack,
Ruth Ann Koster,
Hugh McCorquodale,
Dale Shaddock,
Jack Shaddock*

S.S. No. 9 Holiday School June 1954

*Back row: Sharon Hossack, Sharon Moore, Joan Fortey, Carl Zinn, Noreen Hossack, Hugh McCorquodale, Mrs. West.
3rd Row: Shirley McCall, Marilyn Zinn, Margaret Fortey, Kay Fortey, Ruth Cooper, Ruth Ann Koster,
Linda Fortey, Jane Barker, Julia McGee
2nd row: Linda McWilliams, Joan McWilliams, Beverly McCorquodale, Linda Carey, Joyce Day,
Diane Moore, Susan Barnett, Marie McGee
Front row: David Peel, Bobby Barker, Billy Koster, Billy Goddard, Roy Koster, Robert McWilliams*

S.S. No. 11 McKims P.S. 1954

Teacher: Mrs. Ethel Slater
Back Row: Colin Kittmer, Ray Oakes, Wayne Archer, Jim Pickering, Margaret Baker, Ross Clarke, Egbert Voss
Third Row: Sheila Kittmer, Bob Stewart, Lee McCutcheon, Jo-Ann Stewart, Catherine Wittig, Georgina Mills, Klassia Voss
Second Row: Donald Gregory, Kirby Baker, Joe Pickering, Alan Kittmer, George Pickering, Antone Voss
Front Row: Katherine Gregory, Leonard Pickering, John Muir, Ronald Pickering,
Scott Graff, Faye McCutcheon, Lynne Fader.

S.S. No. 9 Holiday School June 1956

Back row: Miss Golding, Jane Barker, Julia McGee, Dale Shaddock, Sharon Shaddock, Hugh McCorquodale, Sharon Moore, Ruth Koster, Ruth Cooper, Bill Koster.
3rd Row: Mary Koster, Bev McCorquodale, Susan Barnett, Joyce Day, Bill Goddard, Robert McWilliam, Linda Carey, Marie McGee, Ronnie Cooper, George McCall
2nd row: Iva Moore, Joan McWilliam, Diane Moore, Marilyn Zinn, Shirley McCall, Roy Koster, Bobby Barker, Linda McWilliam.
Front row: Jim Day, Barbara McCall, Alma Koster, Bryan Barnett, Mark McWilliam, Patsy Carey, Beth Thornton

S.S. No. 11 McKims P.S. 1957

Back Row: Ron Pickering, Donald Gregory, Colin Kittmer, Joe Pickering, Allan Kittmer, Georgina Mills, George Pickering, Sheila Kittmer, Faye Stewart
Second Row: Ron King, Warren Graff, Brian Pickering, Bob Muir, Lynne Fader, Katherine Gregory, Denis Gregory, Barb Langdon, Larry Archer
Front Row: Leonard Pickering, Scott Graff, Doug Fader, John Muir, Bob Stewart, Charles Kittmer

S.S. No. 9 Holiday P.S. 1957

Mary Babb (teacher) Back row: Marie McGee, Roy Koster, Jane Barker, Julia McGee, Ruth Cooper,
Ruth Ann Koster, Shirley McCall, Bill Koster, Diane Moore
3rd Row: George Thornton, Margaret McCall, Mark McWilliam, Patsy Carey, George McWilliam,
Lynda McWilliam, George McCall, Iva Moore, Barb McCall, Beth Thornton
2nd row: Joan McWilliam, Joyce Day, Billy Goddard, Bobby Barker, Linda Carey, Robert McWilliam,
Susan Barnett, Bev McCorquodale, Mary Koster
Front row: Mary McWilliam, Norman Koster, Ron Cooper, Alma Koster, Brian Barnett, Jim Day, Sharon McCorquodale

S.S. No. 11 McKims P.S. 1958-59

S. S. # 11 E. NISSOURI RURAL SCHOOL
1958-59

Top Row: Lloyd 'Pat' Pickering, Ron King, Charles Kittmer, Sheila Kittmer, Warren Graff,
Dennis Gregory, Faye McCutcheon, Betty-Ann Langdon
Second Row: Larry Archer, Brian Pickering, Doug Fader, Lynn Fader, Scott Graff,
Barry Kittmer, Doug Kittmer, Jim King
Third Row: Barbara Langdon, Bob Stewart, Georgina Mills, Bob Muir, Bob Johnson, John Muir,
Colin Kittmer, George Pickering.
Front Row: Donald Gregory, Ron Pickering, Leonard Pickering, Katherine Gregory, Alan Kittmer.
Teacher: John Hawkesworth.

S.S. No 4 Kintore Kindergarten 1965

Nellie Slater and to her right Randy Brown, Barry Pearson, Brian Cucksey, Mathew Luckhart, Michael Sims, Gavin Stewart, Craig Green, David Older, Daniel Brunsdon, Richard McKeller, Timothy Robson, Roger Quinn, Lori MacDonald, Loraine McDonald, Gail Walters, Heather Heron

AJ Baker Grade 6, 7, 1966-1967

Mrs. Jean Christopher (teacher) Back row: Larry Hogg, Jimmy Sims, Ken Pearson, Billy Harkes, Gerald Mills, John Brunston, Gerald Alderson, Don Pearson, Doug Kennedy, Brian Ball
Middle row: Paul McWilliam, Keith Henderson, Gail Richards, Leisel Cording, Kersten Heron, Barbara Older, Betty Older, Joyce Moore, Eddie McCready, Bruce Brown
Front row: Barb Alderson, Karen Hogg, Muriel Kew, Vivian Day, Janice Alderson, Marilyn Moore, Linda Barnett, Susan Landsdell, Robin Griffon

AJ Baker Staff 1968-1969

Miss Chipps, Miss Rinn, Mrs. Carruthers, Mr. Myers,
Mr. Delbridge, Miss McKay, Mrs. Janet Uren

A.J. Baker Public School Grade 8, 1968-69

Teacher – Mr. Meyers
Back Row: Bruce Brown, Eddie McCready, Theo McCready, Brian Ball, John Anghern, Ken Pearson,
Ken McCorquodale, Keith Henderson, Larry Hogg, Paul McWilliam
Middle Row: Linda Barnett, Marilyn Moore, Gail Richards, Vivian Day, Nancy Holden, Karen Hogg
Front Row: Barb Alderson, Susan Landsdell, Janice Alderson, Debbie Johnson, Suzanne Davies?,
Muriel Kew, Susan Cucksey. Absent: Joyce Mills and Doug Kennedy

Wildwood Park P.S. 1978-1979

Back Row: Mrs. Mainprize (teacher) Barbie Muir, Tommy Ebert, Scott Bolton, Kim Wood, Lynn Worte,
Steven Arthur, Paul Ebert, Bryan Vanoostveen
Second Row: Tony Forman, Nicole Salter, Melanie Bridge, Jackie Guthro, Julie Hopson,
Jackie Hammond, Julie Richardson, Maxine Lewis, Kathy Pringle
Front Row: Danny Hunter, Ricky Bellaire, Shawn King, Kathy Hogg, Brian Vandaele, Sherry Kittmer, Jane Kittmer.
Absent: Timmy Newell, Sherry Rounds, Paula Whittaker

Wildwood Park P.S. Grade 2 and 3, 1979-1980

Back row: Mrs. Mainprize (teacher) Kristina Tate, Nicole Salter, Paula Whittaker, Sherry Rounds,
Cheryl Daniels, Barbie Muir, Jennie Torbet, Charlene Pickering
Middle row: Debbie Bellaire, Suzie Cubberley, Greg Whittaker, Karen Robenburg, Sonya Arthur,
Travis Oakes, Mark McEwan, Scott Barrows, Scott Greason
Front row: Tony Forman, John Bolton, John Squire, Charles Taylor, Brent Tasker, Gregg Stockdale, Josh Lewis, Tommy Wall
Absent: Lee Ann Hopson, Roddy King, Greg Stevenson

4-H Ontario Celebrates its 100th year

"4-H" first came to Ontario under a different name. A Potato Growing contest was started in Carleton County in 1913, but official recognition is given to the Boys' and Girls' Livestock Club in Waterloo County, organized by District Representative Stanley Knapp in 1915. At about the same time a Girls' Gardening and Canning Club was organized in Carleton County, and the Federated Women's Institute organized the first Girls' Sewing Club. In 1931 the first inter-club competition for Boys' and Girls' Clubs was held, and the Canadian Council on Boys' and Girls' Clubs was formed. One thousand Ontario girls completed "A Simple Cotton Dress", the first project under the "Homemaking Clubs" title, in 1935. Boys' and Girls' Clubs and 4-H Clubs co-existed in Oxford County until 1952 when all became "4-H".

Further changes and developments took place under the Ontario Department of Agriculture, later the Ontario Ministry of Agriculture, Food and Rural Affairs. The Ontario 4-H Council was established in 1988. In 2000 4-H became an independent organization. A new logo was presented by 4-H Canada in 2015, retaining the signature four-leaf clover, supporting the 4 Hs which stand for Head, Heart, Health and Hands.

By whatever name, 4-H has provided programs and opportunities to inspire youth, and give them leadership and hands-on experiences. 4-H members follow the motto "Learn To Do By Doing", and repeat the pledge at every meeting. 4-H volunteers rise to the challenges to grow the future of the program, our communities and

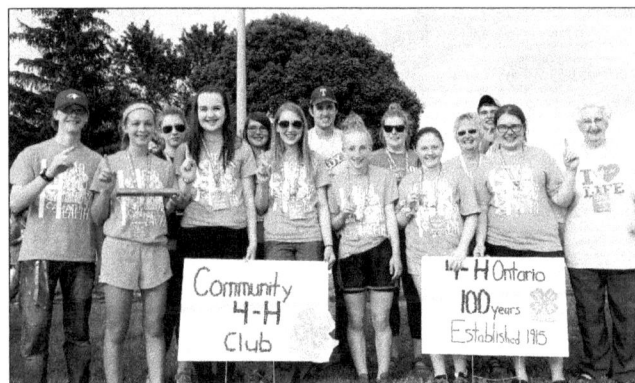

our countries. The structure and requirements of 4-H are those which guided the Boys' and Girls' Clubs.

In Oxford County a number of initiatives have celebrated the anniversary. Our anniversary sign has been on display at businesses and homes throughout the county, and we have participated in local parades, accompanied by enthusiastic members of the 100th Anniversary

Photo taken at the anniversary celebration.

Project. The Oxford 4-H Association supported a special "Artistic Display" class at every fair in the county; members completed a project where they learned to create a display showing some aspect of 4-H, using only natural materials. The fourteen Oxford entries were almost half of the entries in the Artistic Display class at the Royal Agricultural Winter Fair! A celebration dinner was held at Embro Fair, where the theme was "Celebrating 100 Years of 4-H in Ontario". October found more members and volunteers planting 100 trees at Pittock Conservation Area, with the help of the Upper Thames River Conservation Authority, and donations from Cargill Community Care Program, Clark Abbey Memorial funds, George Thornton Bequest funds, Farm Credit Canada, Upper Thames River Conservation Authority/Pittock Conservation Area, an anonymous donor, and the Oxford County 4-H Association.

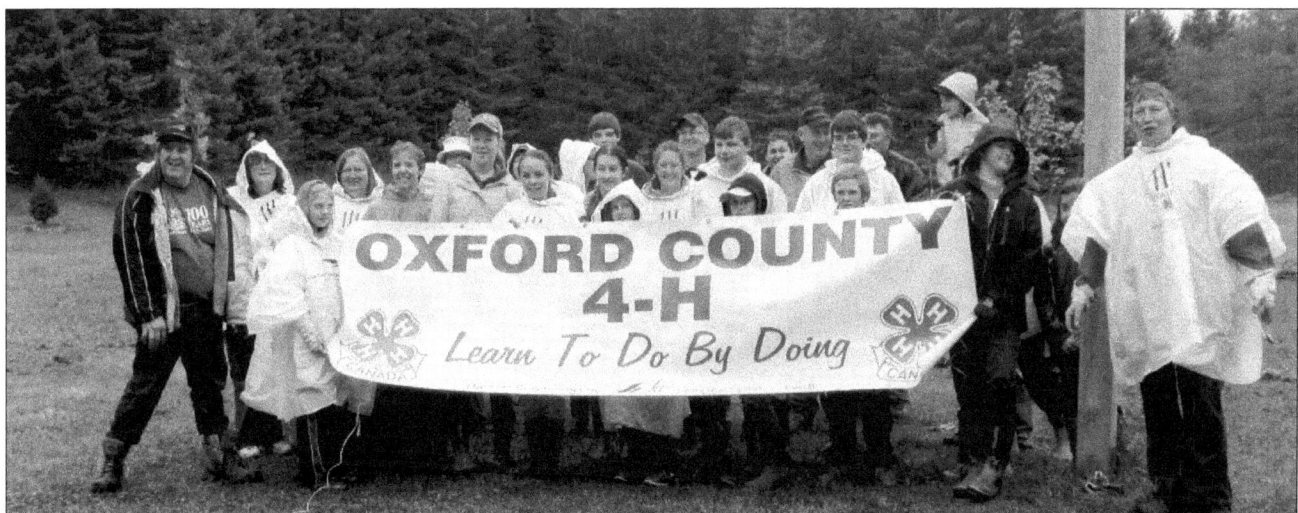

From Zorra Now Winter 2015

Oxford County 4-H has been busy this year celebrating 100 years of 4-H in Ontario throughout the County.

Oxford County 4-H Association sponsored the '4-H Artistic Display' fair class at the 5 Oxford fairs, where Amy Loggan's entry consistently took the top placing. The 14 seed pictures were then taken to the Royal Agricultural Winter Fair in Toronto for the 4-H Artistic Display competition, with Emily Schwartzentruber placing 6th, Amy Loggan 9th, Amy Gras 10th and Hannah Van Boekel 11th out of 30 entries.

Oxford 4-H welcomed 53 new members and 177 returning members for a total of 230 members completing 28 projects in 15 clubs. There were five Dairy clubs (Bennington-Cody's, Bonds, East Nissouri, Ingersoll Kiwanis, Tavistock), whose members participated at various cattle shows in the county and region and at the Royal Agricultural Winter Fair, one Swine Club and two County-wide clubs, one specially formed to spearhead celebrations in the County for the Anniversary of 4-H in Ontario, and one exploring the fun, sportsmanship and safety aspects of Paintball (this one was run as an Oxford - Middlesex collaboration). Six Lifeskills clubs explored projects ranging from cooking, sewing, gardening, drama, heritage, woodworking, crafting, conservation, social recreation, pottery and Lego. Brooksdale offered Explore 4-H – an overview of all things 4-H – The Power of Produce, Lego Engineering, Lego Solar, Wind and Water, and Sew Easy. Embro 2 offered All Manner of Red Meat. Hickson offered Small Engines, the Cookie Club, the Potato Club and a Craft Club featuring Artistic Seed Display – a special class sponsored by Oxford 4-H at fairs in our county. Mt Elgin was busy completing projects on Chocolate, Drama, Woodworking, Our Heritage, and Community Involvement which included blankets made and donated to DASO (Domestic Abuse Services of Oxford) and pillowcases made and donated to the cancer patients at London Sick Kids Hospital. Oxford Centre offered Trash to Treasure and Focus on Fun. Thamesford was able to offer a project on Pottery with support from the FCC 4-H Club Fund. This allowed them to use the facilities of the London Clay Art Centre with assistance from the Potters Guild. They also offered Lego, Social Recreation, A Walk on the Wildside and A World of Food in Canada. As well, the Community Club explored Community Involvement where the members raised over $12,000 for their Relay for Life team. There were 6 teams of Oxford 4-H members participating in the Go For The Gold (trivia game about 4-H projects & local information) competition in July. Two teams advanced to the Regional Go For The Gold in Shedden where one team placed second.

The 2015 4-H Achievement Awards were presented at the Oxford County 4-H Awards Night, November 20, 2015 at the Embro West Zorra Community Center. The evening started with a pot luck dinner and then enjoyed guest speaker Andrew Campbell, who is engaged in using social media for promoting and educating about agriculture while he is busy on the family dairy farm and with various organizations, such as 4-H and other farm-related organizations.

The Gay Lea Awards of Achievement for completing 24 4-H projects and being in 4-H for 5 years were presented by Steve Veldman to Tom Jackson, Trent Jones and Ashley Skillings.

The Janet Wilson Outstanding 4-H Member Awards, sponsored by Woodstock Nursing friends and Janet Wilson memorial funds, were presented by Ross Wilson & family for the Novice female & male—Erin Shrigley / Keeton Jones; Junior female & male—Laura Witmer / Brayden Gras; and Intermediate female & male—Jessie Carberry / Lucas Swartzentruber. The Outstanding Agricultural 4-H Member Award, sponsored by Ontario Plowmen's Association, was presented by Eric Howard to Tanner Jones. The Outstanding Overall 4-H Member Award, sponsored by Your Neighbourhood Credit Union, was presented by Sandra Eedy to Elizabeth Bruce. The Oxford County 4-H Association presented the 30 project completion gift to Julie DeBruyn and Emily Van Bommel, and the 60 project completion certificate to Janneke Van Den Nieuwelaar.

Norman Dickout Memorial Judging Awards were presented by Russell & Bernice Dickout to Novice Olivia Romkes, Junior Lilli Smith, Intermediate Iain Grieve, and Senior & Overall Judging to Josh Karn. The 4-H Project of the Year Award, recognizing the project with the most 4-H participation with activities was presented to the Hickson Cookie 4-H Project members. Recognition and congratulations were given to each member completing 4-H projects in 2015 with a 'Learn To Do By Doing' note pad and year plate. Graduating from the 4-H program after completing 12 years in 4-H are Paul Knoops, Stephanie Koot and Janneke Van Den Nieuwelaar.

Volunteers are an important part of the 4-H program. Recognition of becoming a new 4-H volunteer was given to Julie Schwartzentruber and Carolyn Wilson; completing 5 years to Megan Davis; completing 10 years to Julie McIntosh and Gijs Arts. Karen Witmer, volunteering for 20 years, was given a 4-H Ontario 100th anniversary apron; Marian Sterk, volunteering for 25 years, was given a 4-H spoon custom-made into a bracelet; and a donation was made to the '4-H Forever Legacy Program' to recognize Geoff Innes for 30 years of volunteering.

Recognize any of these 4-Hers?

I PLEDGE
my HEAD
to clearer thinking,
my HEART
to greater loyalty,
my HANDS
to larger service, and
HEALTH
to better living, for

my community,
and my country.

1950's Tavistock Fair

The 4-H Pledge

I pledge
My Head to clearer thinking
My Heart to greater loyalty
My Hands to larger service
My Health to better living
For my Club, my Community,
and my Country.

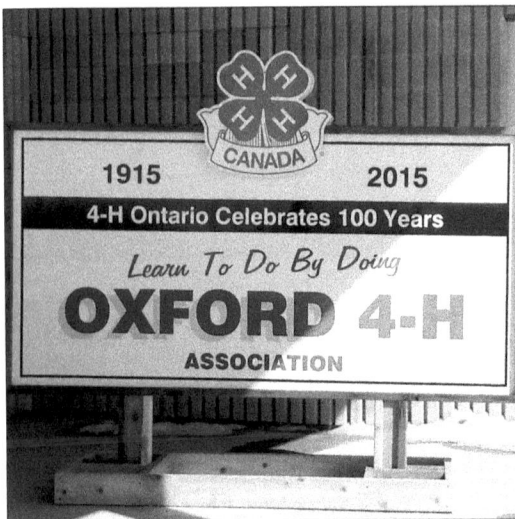

1915   2015
4-H Ontario Celebrates 100 Years
Learn To Do By Doing
OXFORD 4-H
ASSOCIATION

OXFORD COUNTY 4-H "GROW WITH US"

OXFORD COUNTY
4-H
"GROW WITH US"